Angels in Waiting

"Robbie Holz's awareness of Divine Source shines through in her book *Angels in Waiting*. She's captured the true essence of the celestial realm and shares in an easy-to-read manner. This book is a perfect companion to help you see, know, and feel your angels and their light upon your path. A must-read for spiritual awareness!"

MARGARET ANN LEMBO, AUTHOR OF
THE ESSENTIAL GUIDE TO EVERYDAY ANGELS

"*Angels in Waiting* is a gem: pure treasure for seekers who wish for guidance and succor from above. In it, author Robbie Holz shares clear understanding and practical exercises that can bring the reader easily into a place of openness that will allow the angelic assistance that is here for all of us to express in meaningful down-to-earth ways. Accessible and clear, bringing the sacred into daily life, this book will surely be a go-to for many who are on the threshold of awakening to the beauty that is life, the angels, and themselves!"

KATHRYN HUDSON, AUTHOR OF *INVITING ANGELS
INTO YOUR LIFE* AND *DISCOVER YOUR CRYSTAL FAMILY*

"There is great comfort in knowing that there is a guardian angel and a celestial board of advisors assigned to you from birth. One step remains: asking for their help. *Angels in Waiting* shows you exactly how to take that step. Your life is about to change dramatically!"

CHERYL BENTON, FOUNDER AND PUBLISHER OF THE
THREE TOMATOES NEWSLETTER AND AUTHOR OF THE NOVELS
CAN YOU SEE US NOW? AND *CAN YOU HEAR US NOW?*

"This practical book will transform your life. Let *Angels in Waiting* show you, step by step, how to engage powerful help from guardian angels and spirit guides in ways that allow you to overcome struggles and achieve desires."

MAYET LEILANI, MYSTIC, SHAMAN, WRITER, SINGER,
AND MASTER OF CONSCIOUS SOUND

Angels in Waiting

How to Reach Out to Your Guardian Angels and Spirit Guides

Robbie Holz *with* **Judy Katz**

Destiny Books
Rochester, Vermont

Destiny Books
One Park Street
Rochester, Vermont 05767
www.DestinyBooks.com

Destiny Books is a division of Inner Traditions International

Cataloging-in-Publication Data for this title is available from the Library of Congress

ISBN 978-1-64411-316-5 (print)
ISBN 978-1-64411-317-2 (ebook)

Printed and bound in the United States by P. A. Hutchison Company

10 9 8 7 6 5 4 3 2 1

Text design and layout by Priscilla H. Baker
This book was typeset in Garamond Premier Pro with Argent and Trenda used as
display typefaces

To send correspondence to the author of this book, mail a first-class letter to the
author c/o Inner Traditions • Bear & Company, One Park Street, Rochester, VT
05767, and we will forward the communication, or contact the author directly at
www.holzwellness.com.

With love and gratitude to my team
from the other side

Contents

Unlocking the Door to Your Angels

Dear Reader,

In navigating life's many challenges we need all the help we can get. What if I told you that there is tremendous assistance available to you at any time from a celestial source existing in another realm? And that this invisible world, existing alongside our own, is the domain of celestial beings who can be engaged to help you handle life in the best ways possible. My wish for you—my intention in writing this book—is that you recognize the truth of this invisible realm and use this book as a tool to make a connection, so you can use this powerful otherworldly help.

Initially, I was not aware that angels and benevolent spirit guides are always available to assist in every aspect of my life—and yours. Everything moved into high gear for me when in 2000 I met, fell in love with, and eventually married a remarkable man named Gary Holz.

Before Gary came into my life, my personal journey had been a complicated one. Certainly my spiritual awakening had not yet begun in 1985, the year I gave birth to my only child. My son's birth began with a protracted labor that lasted thirty-six exhausting hours and ultimately required a blood transfusion. That transfusion, as it happened, was tainted with hepatitis C, a virus that attacks the liver. That virus lurked passively in my body for seven years before it unleashed its pernicious effects. Then I realized that the birth of my son, the most joyful day of my life, was also the start of a painful odyssey that would twice bring me to the brink of death.

In the years following that toxic transfusion I endured many traditional and cutting-edge experimental treatments by Western medical doctors—all of which failed miserably. No longer able to work, I was bedridden for many months. In addition to the hepatitis C, I now suffered from a host of other ailments, including fibromyalgia, chronic fatigue syndrome, and various severe medical complications triggered by the hepatitis C and the treatments. Ironically, the transfusion of contaminated "life-saving" blood during my labor and delivery had completely destroyed my health.

Having now faced death, first from the hepatitis C and then from the medical doctors' treatments, I found myself confined to my bed and clinging to life. Determined to stay alive long enough for my young son to have memories of me, I relentlessly sought alternative treatment to help my ailing body survive so I could raise my child a little bit longer.

Eventually, to my utter amazement, my desperate search for ways to survive through alternative methods would eventually lead to my transformation in body, mind, and spirit. I completely healed the hepatitis C—which the doctors believed to be incurable at the time—as well as all my other diseases and ailments. That's when I discovered that we are each all-powerful healers! The details of my recovery and spiritual awakening are chronicled in my award-winning memoir, *Aboriginal Secrets of Awakening: A Journey of Healing and Spirituality with a Remote Australian Tribe.* I had survived despite incredible odds. Those experiences opened me up in my early thirties to the bigger questions, which are often ignored unless we are facing death, and sometimes not even then. Through my ordeal, I put traditional religion aside and became intensely spiritual. Suddenly I was on a new and hard-won path.

One day, at a casual summer party in 2000, I met Gary Holz. It was he who first proved to me, without a doubt, that angels are real. Gary was a highly respected, globe-trotting physicist. Despite dealing with the increasingly debilitating effects of multiple sclerosis (MS), he managed to keep his successful business running—that is, until one fateful day when his medical doctors told him to put his affairs in order. They told him that he was close to death due to complications from the MS.

In his quest to heal, Gary went on an incredible journey, alone, into the Australian Outback, to seek out the ancient healing methods of a remote aboriginal tribe. He went there as a quadriplegic confined to a wheelchair, and returned a paraplegic, having regained feeling in his body for the first time in seven years.

While that alone is huge, what he came back with was even more astonishing. The remote aboriginal healers taught this logic-based scientist, who once saw things as black or white, that gray areas do indeed exist even if they cannot be proven. While in the Outback, Gary became aware of his angel, Julie, and began communicating with her.

The aboriginal tribespeople taught Gary their over 60,000-year-old healing principles. They then made an unusual request—that he take their healing secrets out into the world because, they maintained, modern Western medicine didn't truly understand how healing worked—or could work.

Upon returning from the Outback, Gary obtained a Ph.D. in immunology and a master's degree in nutrition to help him garner respect as he called attention to the aboriginal healing techniques he'd been taught and that had done so much for him. Quickly putting all of his newfound understanding and abilities to work, he helped many people transform their lives in the most positive ways. Dr. Gary Holz's own experiences with the aboriginal tribespeople and their healing secrets are well documented in his best-selling memoir, *Secrets of Aboriginal Healing: A Physicist's Journey with a Remote Australian Tribe.*

As I worked side-by-side with Gary, I learned about the communication that he regularly exchanged with his angel, Julie. Like the remote Outback tribespeople, at this point Gary was able to see and hear angels and spirit guides from the other side of the veil. The aboriginal tribespeople had opened Gary up to the existence of unseen benevolent beings, and he was able to do the same for me.

What I learned, which I am now sharing with you, is that at least one guardian angel is assigned to each of us. This entity is at our side from the moment of our first breath until our last breath with our death. Though we may not always feel their presence, these guardian angels have a profound impact on our lives. Often events that we think of as a "lucky break" or a "happy coincidence" are the result of these assigned guardian angels working for us behind the scenes. In truth, the immense love they feel for us is beyond our human comprehension.

It's important to know that their infinite dominion is far more effective and influential if we grant these powerful angels *permission* to enter our lives in more expansive ways. It is vital to *ask* for their help because we live on a free-will planet.

Since 2001 I have been teaching others to make the same connections and requests that Gary taught me to do. As people use the tremendous help available from angels and benevolent spirit guides, their lives are dramatically improved. Watching these transformations take place, I knew I needed to share this vital information widely so many others could also benefit, causing a slow but steady ripple effect in the larger world.

In the following pages I will teach you what you need to know in order for you to be able to deepen your connection with angels and spirit guides and engage their powerful assistance with your struggles and desires. I will show you how to engage their limitless help to find happiness and peace, regardless of what challenges you are presently dealing with.

I am also going to share how I have worked with those who come to me for help in healing physically and emotionally. For obvious reasons I don't use their real names. Some characteristics of their lives have also been changed. Nonetheless, these anecdotes all represent accurate composite portraits of my clients.

The struggles my clients have dealt with and the methods I describe as we move ahead in our work together will make it clear to you how you can appeal to *your* guardian angel—the one granted to you at birth and always working on the sidelines in your behalf. Taking in the experiences of my clients, you will learn how to initiate and nurture your own angelic relationships, how to recognize their guidance, and how to receive the greatest benefit from their support.

This is my promise to you: that in the course of reading this book you will come to understand how to engage powerful help from the angels and spirit guides so that it will enrich your life beyond what you are currently able to accomplish. What you are about to discover is how empowered and enriched your life will become when you engage their assistance.

Are you ready to begin? Please turn the page and open the door to the world of angels and spirit guides.

LOVE,
ROBBIE HOLZ

1

Welcome to
the Celestial Plane

Every visible thing in this world is put under the charge of an angel.

SAINT AUGUSTINE

This is an incredible time to be alive in the history of the world, both for me and for you. Yes, *you specifically,* my dear reader. Reading this statement may have caused you to raise an eyebrow with doubt. And you have good reason to be doubtful. It only takes moments to observe the world around us to become filled with despair. Turn on your television to be greeted by news of ever more horrendous events: terrorists firing their rifles into the cafes of Paris; men with nuclear weapons saber-rattling on the world stage; entrenched widespread poverty impacting the most vulnerable among us. All the while, your smartphone or device beams news of tragedy, corruption, and greed directly into your head. When you look up from that small screen you are greeted with one more alarming sight—a sea of faces intensely locked down, peering into their electronic devices. No wonder the world may seem both a violent and an isolating place.

In your personal world you may have checked your bank balance recently and found the bottom line anxiety-inducing. Or perhaps you have looked in the mirror and suddenly found too many lines and creases, making you wonder where the years have gone, causing you to muse on what's become of the dreams of your youth. You may have caught your partner in bed with someone else. You may have not spoken to your adult children in years. Your boss may have just informed you that the company no longer requires your services. These are just a few of the pitfalls that we humans encounter every day.

Hopefully, none of these trials are currently on your shoulders. But life does present us with unexpected challenges and obstacles, and for many reasons specific to your life you may be feeling a bit lost and hopeless. You may even have read my enthusiastic opening statement and thought, *An incredible time in history to be alive? What is Robbie Holz talking about? Who does she think she is to tell me that this is a wonderful, amazing time to be alive when it seems exactly the opposite?*

On one level, you would be correct: I don't know you or your personal struggles. But what I do know, with every fiber of my being, is that you are emphatically *not* alone in your difficulties. In fact, you are less alone than anyone has been in the history of the world. This is a big statement. However, I also know it is true because of what you most likely do not know right now. It's what I hope will become a certainty in your life by the time you finish reading this book and absorb its important lessons. Namely, that you are surrounded by angels, and that the purpose of these angels is to aid you in times of distress and escort you toward the light. It is important to know that they are most effective when the darkness seems to be closing in around you, or sucking the very air out of your lungs.

We are at a crucial point. Our planet is nearing the end of an era driven by greed, ego, materialism, and negativity of all sorts. Due to this crisis and the nexus of difficulties and confusion, this volunteer army of glorious spirit guides, these angels and celestial advisors, are visiting us in unprecedented numbers.

It is important to understand the nature of angels, who are etheric, immortal beings of light. Angels existed long before this universe began to spin, and they comprehend the precious beauty of existence itself. Angels love you unconditionally for the simple fact of your existence. The angelic presence is here to help you in difficult times and in joyous times. They're here to nudge you along the path to greater awareness and heighten your ability to perceive the world around you with a higher consciousness.

At this moment in time, angels are in the process of bringing about a planetwide awakening. This awakening will reconfigure the consciousness of humanity and increase compassion and service to others, which creates a more love-based existence. Every day, angels spread messages of benevolent goodness that are magnified exponentially with each soul they touch. As they help people awaken to their higher state of being, darkness is slowly but surely receding from this planet. The truth is coming out. Collectively we are moving into light and love on the wings of angels.

Believe it or not, angels have already been helping you, even if you've never even *thought* about an angel before now. When you actively engage with them, something they eagerly desire, they have so much more to offer you. I can state without reservation that when you do reach out to your angels and spirit guides, it will shatter your preconceptions of what you think is possible. Of course, I will explain how to make contact with these beings. First, though, you will need to understand the spirit realm in greater depth. In short, you are about to embark on a "starter course" in the divine.

So now, I invite you to open yourself up, heart and soul, to the angelic realm. I know you're going to like what you see.

THE MISSION OF ANGELS ON EARTH

Perhaps you have always had a sense, or a feeling, that some higher presence was a part of your life. Perhaps you are even well-informed about angels. Despite your experience, a flurry of questions may be flooding your mind right now. Let's begin with the most basic: If there are angels, why would they interact with human beings? Why would they want to be involved with humankind at all?

As is often the case, the most important questions have remarkably simple answers. Angels come to Earth to serve humanity. It is our right to ask for and receive their assistance. They are here to help us express divine qualities such as love, forgiveness, and compassion.

It is helpful to understand that angels, because they are altruistic beings, do not have the same level of free will that humans do. But they do not view their lack of free will—which inhibits them from any action that does not serve humanity—in a negative context. Instead, they understand that their immortality and their unlimited consciousness is a blessing. Being of service to those who can exercise free will is an important aspect of being.

As a human you have the ability to create whatever kind of life you desire, whether it is one of goodness that will lead you toward happiness, or one of negativity that causes earthly misery for you and others. This is both your magnificent gift and your cross to bear. Angels lack the paradox of free will—they have only positive gifts to bestow. Thus, every action they take is a noble and virtuous one, granted by the Eternal Being.

By their very nature, benevolent angels are unable to do harm, so you never need fear them nor doubt any of their communications. They have no ulterior motives or hidden agendas. And they are the antithesis of some mythical trickster in a fairy tale that pretends to offer help and later claims your soul as payment. You can always trust angels because they are unable to lie. You are always completely safe with angels because they are unable to cause you harm.

The great news is that you have untold numbers of these totally magnanimous beings watching over you at all times. You are never out of their reach. You can never stray from their protection. Isn't that a wonderful, comforting thought? Angels are in your world to sustain, support, and uplift you. Nurturing you is in their very essence. I have to say: you and I are so blessed that these beautiful beings are part of our world!

Once you learn to understand the nature of angels, you can then begin to know that angels can help you in nearly limitless ways. They are able to lift your energy to a more peaceful one. If you're feeling depressed, you can call on an angelic presence and ask for help to change your state of mind. If you are feeling uncertain of your path, they will help you find clarity, if you ask. They may skillfully guide you to find an answer to a problem. Their presence moves through your world unobtrusively. It is never their intention that you become dependent on their guidance. If you let them, however, they will give you so much more than you ever imagined possible.

DISCOVERING YOUR POWERFUL TEAM

In my initial explanation of the angelic realm, I have used the word *angel* as an umbrella term for the many benevolent spiritual forces that surround us. I'll now be more specific about the different types of celestial beings that exist, and I'll explain the individual gifts they bestow on us. Although there are nearly boundless forms that celestial entities can take, the most common on our earthly plane are these: angels, guardian angels, and archangels.

Before I describe a few types of celestial beings and their specific role, it is important to remember one crucial point. It is vital not to think of angels as singular beings that visit Earth with a specific mission. Rather, angels exist as part of a massive celestial squadron, and they are always in contact with one another. You have access to as many members of this squadron as you want, and they will, in turn, form your "team" of spiritual forces. Every member of your team brings something unique to the table, and each one is able to communicate with the other team members. As an example, if you appeal to an angel for help and that angel feels a different guide is better equipped for the task, they will call on another guide to step in.

You may be wondering: Why all the specialization? If angels are perfect beings, why are so many of them needed to help me? Here is the answer: Angels understand that because of biological evolution, the human mind thinks in structured patterns. In the angelic kingdom there are no levels. But we humans generally need a hierarchy to be able to feel comfortable and at ease with the presence of angels, so they provide us with one. Incidentally, this fact of human-celestial interaction does not matter to them at all. They know we humans need a label to identify our angels, some name to call them, some structured order that makes sense to us, so they give it to us.

They don't look down on us for thinking in these organized ways. They understand that our minds are at a stage that requires hierarchies. Hence they allow us to maintain our accustomed way of thinking because to do otherwise would hijack our free will. It is vital that humanity's free will remain intact.

The predominant member of your spiritual team is a *guardian angel*. Your guardian angel responds first to your needs and requests. Guardian angels are designed to be the easiest for you to communicate with on your team. Every person on Earth has at least one guardian angel assigned to him or her, a divine entity who is at your side throughout the course of your life. Guardian angels are here to guide, support, and protect you *in accordance with your soul's desires.*

They assist in your growth and evolvement. Guardian angels also prevent you from being harmed, killed, or exposed to things your soul does not intend you to experience. One or more of your angels have probably saved you many times without you even knowing it. Have you ever experienced a near miss from an automobile accident, or stepped into the street just as a bus whizzed by, only to be pulled back by a stranger?

Your guardian angel is supported by a team of various other angels. These angels assist in matters small and large, and can be called on when needed. Unlike your guardian angel, they weren't assigned to you directly but are part of your team. Once you engage their help, your life will change for the better, and over time you will add more and more to your team of spiritual forces who are eager, willing, and able to help you to ultimately enhance your life.

Among the most powerful of the angelic forces are the *archangels*. In fact, every major religion—Christianity, Islam, Judaism, Buddhism, and Hinduism—has a tradition of angels and archangels that is intrinsic to their belief systems. Archangels are mighty beings who act as celestial generals.

The names and roles of these archangels vary from tradition to tradition, but in the Christian tradition there are seven original archangels—Michael, Gabriel, Raphael, Uriel, Simiel, Oriphiel, and Raguel. The suffix *el* at the end of each name means "of god" in Hebrew. These archangels are some of the oldest and most powerful beings in the universe. Each archangel has a specialty. Archangel Michael, with his sword, is a protector. Call on Michael when you are feeling unsafe or vulnerable. Archangel Raphael is a healer and works with Mother Mary (Queen of the Angels) in the healing realm. Archangel Gabriel is known as the "messenger" angel. Gabriel helps you with your life's purpose, communication, creativity, and expressing your talent.

While angels do not incarnate as humans, there are members of your spiritual forces team who have, such as Ascended Masters, spirit guides, and deceased loved ones. *Spirit guides* were formerly humans that have transitioned to the other side of the veil, the afterlife. They have achieved a high level of enlightenment. A spirit guide chooses to remain as a disembodied spirit in order to be of service as a guide and protector to a living human. They remain close to humanity in order to help and guide us—particularly in this transformational time. While some spirit guides remain by your side, others come and go depending on your needs. You may have several spirit guides at the same time.

It should be noted that we are *only* working with benevolent beings from the other side of the veil. Needless to say, we do not engage malevolent beings of darkness.

Also available to you are the *Ascended Masters*. An Ascended Master is someone who has lived many lifetimes as a human and undergone profound spiritual transformation. Although not every Ascended Master has experienced many reincarnations, they have each attained a highly enlightened state. They are beings of love and light who vibrate at a higher frequency than even archangels. There are many Ascended Masters, but some names you might recognize include St. John the Baptist, Buddha, Mohammed, Mother Mary, and Mary Magdalene.

Mary Magdalene, the companion of Jesus, is a key member of my personal spiritual team. She has been instrumental in the creation of this book. Magdalene has assured me that her powerful energy will be coming from this book to help readers awaken. Perhaps you feel that energy now. Magdalene and I have a strong connection. We work together to help humankind. I'm the "boots on the ground" human member of the team; she's the Ascended Master directing me from the other side.

Your deceased loved ones and ancestors may become part of your spiritual forces team. They may assist you whether you knew them during their lifetime or not. Feel free to ask for their assistance since you will not be keeping them from other things as they can do many things at the same time in multiple dimensions.

We tend to think of deceased loved ones and family members as spirit guides. While they may guide, help, and protect you, they are not technically categorized as spirit guides. They have not yet reached the level of mastery and high frequency of spirit guides. Think of spirit guides as university professors and your departed loved ones as primary school teachers.

REALIZING THE LIMITS OF YOUR RATIONAL MIND

If you are like some people you are willing to be open-minded, but when confronted by information about angels the logical part of your brain wants to put on the brakes. Comedian George Carlin once compared a belief in angels to a belief in ghosts and goblins. Several atheistic philosophers have made similar, less colorful arguments seem logical. You know what? They're right; at least on a rational level, angels don't make sense, not as we understand it. For them, there are limits to the rational mind, but I have no interest in relying solely on my rational mind. Life isn't a class in debate or rhetoric, where you are graded on how clever you are. There is no test at the end, and you don't get bonus points for being cynical about the supernatural. I have thought long and hard as to whether my belief in the celestial realms is logical. But once I saw what my celestial protectors meant in my life, my days of doubt ended forever.

I'm not suggesting that you totally abandon your good judgment or common sense. You need a cautious and logical mind to see things with clarity to navigate your day-to-day life. At the same time you should never allow your logical mind to override your intuition. Intuition is the precious tool that allows you to know something to be true without conscious reasoning. In other words, intuition is your inner wisdom.

Your mind is a very influential tool but it was never designed to be in charge. The human mind is intended to be the servant of the soul. Your mind can help you solve everyday problems, but it doesn't know the best way to achieve a fulfilling career, find a high-quality partner, or be an excellent parent. But these *are* things that your higher consciousness, your soul, and your angels absolutely do know!

Swiss Protestant theologian Walter Nigg (1903–1988), who wrote extensively on saints and angels, echoed this belief when he wrote, "Angels are powers which transcend the logic of our existence." British poet, critic, and philosopher Samuel Taylor Coleridge (1772–1834) expressed a similar belief when he wrote, "The world has angels all too few, and heaven is overflowing." Coleridge believed too that we must open our minds to achieve a "willing suspension of disbelief in order to drink the milk of paradise."

The current state of our world reflects what happens when the rational mind is allowed to control everything and take precedence over the soul's true wisdom. Today, many people are not listening to the guidance from their soul and spend their days and nights allowing their minds to entertain idle thoughts that spin away in their busy brains. Our ego-driven minds take over, abuse us, deceive us, and use us. Many of us have unwittingly allowed ourselves to become slaves to what we, and society, consider our "logical" minds.

This insanity is like a chronic malaise that our culture now considers normal. Think of the chronic conditions that plague humankind: obesity, depression, and opioid addictions are only a few among the myriad signs of societal dysfunction. Rather than discover the source of our issues we make clothing in larger sizes and create easier access to alcohol and mind-numbing chemical substances. Clearly, logic only goes so far. We need to get back to our spiritual roots.

By existing only on the mental and material plane, without a spiritual component in your life, you are missing the key ingredient in the recipe for happiness and fulfillment. To allow the spiritual component to enter your consciousness, you need to let go of your ego-driven mind and embrace the spiritual dimension. We are all familiar with how ego operates in others, and in ourselves, but the *ego,* from the ancient Greek for "I am" or "I exist," only creates a false sense of self. Whenever you are in a dark place and your first impulse is to close yourself off, know that *that* is the perfect time to relinquish your egoic control and open yourself up to spiritual guidance. Then you can allow the celestial beings assigned to you to shine their healing light on your wounded spirit and infuse you with renewed energy and optimism.

When something inside tells you that you *should, must,* or *have* to do something, know that it's your mind or ego talking. And all those thoughts are coming from a place of deep fear that you might not even acknowledge: a fear that is trying to control you. In contrast, when you are directed by gut instinct or intuition, when something *feels* right, know that this guidance is coming from your higher self or higher consciousness. Think of it as a whisper coming from your guardian angel or benevolent spirit guide. Best of all, know that their guidance is based on love.

Along this journey, I want you to continually strip away the distortions of your egoic mind. This mind wants you to believe you are not part of the Oneness, that you are separate from Divine Source and from everyone else. This false notion of separateness is why it's important to start monitoring your thoughts rather than allowing your thoughts to rule you. You can take control of your mind by being more conscious, mindful, present, and by becoming aware of what your mind is doing. The alternative is to continue to allow your mind to have its way with you, by habitually engaging in fearful, negative thoughts.

At first, you might find that observing your own thoughts is a new and daunting process, yet it is essential. We are all in the habit of thinking, *I'm not good enough,* but it's not true; that's simply a thought. You must become an objective *observer* of your thoughts and not permit yourself to be automatically pulled into your mind's customary distorted thinking. Too many of us are on autopilot and at the mercy of our mind's whims. It's time for that to stop!

If you are able to observe and then control your bossy rational mind with detachment, you'll be able to let go of a lot of the painful aspects of your life. You'll no longer be tied to your superficial identity, no matter what label you wear, be it wife, daughter, teacher, husband, addict, lawyer, brother, worker, depressive, anorexic, etc. These are just conditioned beliefs, distortions created by your mind. It's not who you really are. It is just a story you tell yourself.

We're not on Earth to adhere to these limiting beliefs. We're here to wake up to the mind's tricks, to strip away its identity and distorted sense of who we are. When you do that, you will discover your true essence: a divine being, comprised of Divine Source, connected to the universal Oneness and to everything and everyone.

I'm about to tell you more about yourself.

YOUR SOUL AND THE DIVINE SPIRIT WITHIN

It is imperative to understand that you don't *have* a soul; you *are* a soul. This is a critical distinction. The soul is not a separate entity from the self. In truth, the human soul is the epitome of creative expression, with unlimited free will. You should think of Earth as a paradise and a school for souls where your spirit, in human form, experiences the gifts of a physical body and the blessings of a wider range of human emotions.

A soul is an eternal, etheric spirit that inhabits the body and acts through it. It is like the hand in a puppet, the astronaut inside the spacesuit. When the hand (soul) is removed, the puppet (body) collapses. When a person physically dies, the soul leaves the body but continues as an eternal spirit in a dimension of a higher frequency, what some refer to as heaven. Your soul encapsulates the wisdom of many, many lifetimes. It is your soul's deep desire to grow and evolve toward love. That is why a soul chooses to incarnate over and over again. It uses one body after another for growth, enlightenment, and expression of its true divine nature.

For an etheric spirit to inhabit a physical form is a tremendous gift. Once I asked one of my spirit guides what she missed about being in a physical body. You'll never guess what she told me. She said she missed a "good sneeze" and the "miracle of watching a wound heal." Living in these miraculous bodies, we take a lot for granted.

Although our minds may vehemently disagree, having a wide range of emotions is also an incredible blessing. This broad spectrum of emotions enables us to experience feelings not felt on the other side of the veil, like jealousy, impatience, and anger. Everything is in perfection on the other side of the veil, which makes it stagnant for growth purposes. We learn and grow more through adversities and challenges. Fear-based emotions enable us to recognize where our mind resists responding with love. The difference between toxic emotions and love-based emotions enables us to see things more clearly, just as contrasts in a painting provide greater definition.

Earth is a school for souls. The extreme diversities of darkness and light provide limitless opportunities for growth. We need both shadow and light on the planet and within us—through our thoughts and emotions—to realize when we are controlled by our minds or responding from our loving divine nature. The physical body and emotions are necessary tools for Earth school. The body and emotions are connected and reflective of each other. Cherish your body and embrace all your emotions. They are necessary components of reaching enlightenment.

Enrolled in this challenging school on this free-will planet, our souls choose what to experience. They decide what to gain mastery over and how. Their pace and methods are determined by their current level of soul growth. Less-evolved souls may choose to learn foundational basics like materiality, greed, or vanity. More-evolved souls may explore greater acceptance, service to others, or deeper compassion.

We are all equal as souls. We are in different classrooms depending on our level of soul evolvement. A graduate with a master's degree in physics would not judge a first grader learning math fundamentals. It is paramount not to judge others in their earlier stages of growth.

Your soul chooses your body, characteristics, and family. You are the way you need to be for your soul's purposes in this incarnation. This journey will reflect what your soul intends for you to master. If your soul wants you to attain greater self-love, it may put a plan in place with family and society conditioning you to believe you are not good enough or loveable. Your soul intends for you to eventually overcome these misconceptions and find love from within rather than outside of you.

Ultimately, you will realize you are a fractal of Divine Source, known by many names like God, Goddess, Creator, Eternal Being. If you think of Divine Source as the ocean, you are not a drop in the ocean but the entire ocean in a drop. You are the exact same quality of Divine Source but a small quantity. Divine Source explores and expresses through you. You are Divine Source experiencing life as an incarnated soul in a human body.

Understanding Divine Source is crucial to your perception of yourself as a godly being. Scientists have proven that even at its smallest element, everything has the same seed of life. You are one with all of life because everything, at its most basic level, is comprised of this Divine Source. We are just separated into different expressions. Once you understand this, you realize that everything in existence—from the tallest tree, to the smallest bug, to the endless galaxy—is a different form of Divine Source. This Divine Source simply wants to *be*. Right now it is exploring, expressing, and creating through you in human form. Every being who is incarnated in a living body on planet Earth is divine, make no mistake about it.

As we continue on this journey, I want you to keep the takeaways from this chapter centered in your heart:

- Angels are on this plane to help you.
- You always have a powerful team of angels at the ready, led by your guardian angel.
- Benevolent spirit guides, Ascended Masters, and deceased loved ones are also available to help you.
- Your rational mind needs to give way to your intuitive mind.
- You are inherently divine because you are comprised of Divine Source.

Next I will show you how to actively communicate with your spiritual forces team. Like long-lost relatives, they are always excited to hear from you.

⌒⌒

2

Interacting with the
Spirit World

*When angels visit us, we do not hear the rustle of wings,
nor feel the feathery touch of the breast of a dove; but we
know their presence by the love they create in our hearts.*

MARY BAKER EDDY

ᕼᕯ

J am aware that right now you, my dear reader, may be reacting
to the previous chapter with a mixture of excitement, frustration, and anticipation. After all, I have taken great care to describe a
marvelous spirit realm whose purpose is to help *you,* but I have not
yet shown you how to contact the realm.

Robbie Holz, I can hear you saying, *I need to know how to reach
out to my angels and spirit guides. I've got more than a few problems I
could surely use their help with.*

Fear not, I will not leave you in the lurch. But before we get
started I want to emphasize one pivotal point, a point that if
ignored will greatly impede your progress. Communicating with

these other realms is a process. Contacting angels and guides is not a matter of raising your face toward heaven and asking—even earnestly *pleading*—for assistance. All your problems will not be magically solved with the stroke of an angelic wand.

However, if you take the process of "reaching out" seriously and learn to view it as a series of steps, I promise you it will yield exponential results that will impact your life in many positive ways. In fact, ideally you will not only trust the process, but delight in it and find joy in your progress.

Like any other long and important journey, embracing higher-frequency beings such as angels and spirit guides begins with a single step. First, you must open up to the most powerful being in your celestial team, your guardian angel, because it all begins with awareness of your chief protector in the angelic kingdom.

REACHING OUT TO YOUR
GUARDIAN ANGEL

As you know—and will fully experience for yourself—you have your own personal guardian angel, a being that has watched over you since the moment you were born. It should be an enormously comforting thought that you're never without access to this angelic being. *Never!* Your guardian angel is telepathic to all your thoughts. Asking in your mind for their help is all you need to do to engage their assistance. Don't complicate it. It's incredibly easy. Asking once in your mind is all they need. Your thoughts will always bring their presence front and center, but first you must ask.

The key word here is exactly that: *ask*. Unfortunately, angels, even your specific guardian angel, cannot just announce themselves. You have to actively engage them by asking for their help. Angels are in your life to be of service, but you must invite them to take part in your life. They respect your free will far too much to simply intrude into your world uninvited.

That does not mean that your guardian angel hasn't been keeping an eye on you. In fact, quite the contrary is true. Have you ever tripped and fallen to the ground only to get up and find that you are perfectly fine? That's likely an intervention by your guardian angel. Have you ever found yourself drowsy while driving, and dangerously drifting into another lane, when you are suddenly wide awake and able to swerve back into safety just as an enormous truck blew past you? Guess who? Your life, my life, and all our lives are filled with such incidences, which I will call "noncoincidences."

You may be eager to begin the initial "ask" and feel the full light of your guardian angel. But before I show you how to initiate this conversation—a conversation that will significantly alter the course of your existence—you must be sure you are mentally prepared. So first, let's do a mindfulness exercise that will prepare you for experiencing your guardian angel.

Find a tranquil place where you feel secure and comfortable. It should have some personal significance. Perhaps it's a table where you have eaten lovely meals with your family, a place of worship, or even just a quiet room where you will not be disturbed. It can be somewhere in public, like a bench in the park or a blanket on the beach, as long as there are not too many people in your vicinity. Ideally you will be alone.

Once settled, close your eyes and picture everything in your life that you associate with your sense of self. Thoughts will begin to fly around in your mind: your family, your work, a friend or partner who may have recently gotten on your nerves, your to-do lists. Some of these things might seem vital to your core self while others might seem shockingly trivial. That isn't important since self-judgment is not wanted here.

What's important is to let these thoughts, impressions, and pictures wash over you like waves. Visualize these thoughts as ocean

waves washing up on the shore while you stand waist-deep in the
surging tide. Can you feel this endless parade of unbidden thoughts
rising and falling around you? Can you feel them beginning to pile up,
pulling you further out, making you feel as though you are in danger
of drowning?

Now step out of the waist-high seawater. Feel the warm sand
under your feet as you free yourself from the torrent of unwanted
thoughts and impressions. Look at all those things rushing by. Even
more random thoughts may come—perhaps the faces of your children
or parents—but now that you are back on land, safe and warm, you
can watch them float away. These impressions are outside of your
essence now—they are simply the ornaments of existence.

Now ask yourself: What am I left with? What have I brought
with me onto the shore? Your thoughts and emotions are, in reality,
not you, but rather the building blocks of your consciousness. How do
you really feel about who you are on a soul level? Excavate the deep
recesses of your being, pulling forth truth from a place that only you
know exists or that no one aside from you can change or corrupt. Begin
to imagine that you are standing in the light of truth and that truth,
like rays of sunlight, are warming and drying your damp skin. That's
your divine essence shining through—an essential part of your being.

It can be enormously difficult, even frightening, to confront ourselves on a soul-deep level, to illuminate parts of our minds we have
allowed to become dark and fallow. However, I didn't subject you to
this exercise without good reason. I wanted to show you how we often
define ourselves too broadly by external factors. That's why many of
the first things—thoughts and images—that jump into the mind are
just that: *things.* Those external concepts are not your true divine self.

Now let's turn our attention to communicating with the angels
and spirit guides. It's important to know that when you talk to angels
and guides in your mind, they hear you telepathically. Your per-

sonal guardian angel is aware of *every single thought you have*. Every thought, be it a little flight of fancy or a huge epiphany, is transmitted in full directly to your guardian angel. Since this is the case, it's only natural that the way to begin your "ask" to your guardian angel is through your thoughts. If you specifically direct your thoughts to your guardian angel, you will let that compassionate, loving entity know you are trying to communicate directly—that you want them to enter your consciousness in an entirely new and exciting way.

INTENTION IS THE KEY

To communicate your thoughts to your guardian angel, you need to have an *intention*. Make it clear that it is your intention for your guardian angel to be a larger, more active presence in your life. Once you set that intention through your thoughts, then simply tell them that you need their help, and be specific about what sort of help you need.

Over time you will develop a closer and more satisfying connection with your guardian angel. Spend time with them as you would with a friend. Get to know them. Provide yourself with a quiet environment where you can sit with your intention and call forth your guardian angel. Ask that they be with you in a more conscious way. Thank them for their presence. Persistence and consistency are key. You can't do this just once every few months. You can't develop a close relationship with another human being if you only see or hear from them every six months or so. The closer you are in this relationship with your guardian angel, the more you will benefit from it.

Angelic relationships resemble human ones. The difference is that your guardian angel will never let you down or betray you in any way. Humans might lie to you or cheat you, but benevolent angels are quite literally incapable of such negative qualities. Your guardian angel's purpose is to guide you through your human experience, helping your divine essence shine through more and more each day.

Once you've established a thought-based relationship with your guardian angel, you can begin asking for more help with specific matters. Never feel like you're asking for too many things—remember, the angels' mission is to aid us, and your guardian angel's purpose is to aid *you*. You can ask for help with anything and everything in your daily life, big or small, specific or general.

You can ask your guardian angel to help you *live the highest vision of your soul*. You can also ask for smaller things, such as the courage to try something new, or the strength to forgive someone. You may also ask for help with the simplest of things in life. It doesn't have to be a crisis. They can help you with your next exam. They can help you when you don't know how to communicate with someone. They can raise the vibrations in you, causing your general mood to improve.

The relationship with your guardian angel is truly a symbiotic one. It may be easier to ask for help if you realize that every time your guardian angel assists, it enables them to grow because they are serving you out of tremendous love. In truth, you and your guardian angel are in a cooperative, mutually beneficial relationship. This is true for the other members of your spirit team as well. Because they are serving you out of immense love, every time you ask and allow their help, they evolve. As you grow, they grow.

As you focus on your guardian angel, you will become more aware of angels and spirit guides and the impact they have on your life. Of course this takes time and requires some patience. But eventually this will become second nature, and you and your guardian angel and other members of your spirit team will be functioning as a well-oiled unit. At this early stage in your relationship with your guardian angel don't become frustrated with yourself or your guardian angel. Keep reaching out with intention, and soon miraculous things will happen.

RECOGNIZE GUIDANCE FROM
ANGELS AND SPIRIT GUIDES

Connecting with your guardian angel is only the beginning of a lifelong relationship. It's one that will function differently than any other relationship you've had in the past. Clearly, you're going to have to learn how to identify communications from these beings from higher dimensions and apply these messages to your life. Guidance from your spirit team won't always come in forms that feel recognizable or familiar. Receiving their messages isn't as simple as picking up a phone and listening to someone's instructions. You're going to have to learn how to discern nonverbal and soul-level transmissions from the angels and guides.

The best way to start recognizing your guardian angel's signs is to release any preconceived beliefs about how they are going to manifest to you. This special angel-to-human communication takes time to develop. These signs of contact most likely won't come in the form of glorious visions or voices booming from above, although that is possible. It's not very common, but some people are clairaudient or clairvoyant and can actually *hear* or *see* angelic guidance. Most likely your experience will be subtler, but that doesn't mean it's not just as powerful and special. Sometimes the most valuable lessons are those that are softly whispered.

Truly listening to your soul-level consciousness is going to be one of the most valuable tools in your toolbox when it comes to identifying angelic guidance. Be quiet for a few minutes each day and intuitively feel the messages being transmitted to you. If your mind insists there's no time, ignore those negative messages. Be intentional and make peaceful respites for yourself throughout the day to listen, even if only for brief moments. Always remember to *ask* for what you need, identifying your problem so that your guardian angel can help you solve it.

Over time, my clients have often reported that their guardian's voice resembles something closer to intuition and a sense of inner knowing rather than an actual spoken voice. Everyone is clairsentient, where you *feel* angelic guidance and communication within your body, especially in the chest area. And you can feel it in your core. Listen to how your heart feels, and then begin to accept and validate those feelings. Above all, don't question them.

Although everyone's journey is unique, I've detailed a few of the ways your spirit team may convey its messages to you. These are signs that people have consistently reported to me over the years, and I have experienced many of them personally. They are things to look for or methods you can employ to enhance your connection with angels and spirit guides. Some of these signs include:

- Finding specific objects like feathers or coins, or feeling a spontaneous gentle breeze are just a few ways angels and guides signal their presence and say hello.
- Computer glitches, a broken pen, a dropped phone call are some of the different ways your team may use to interrupt your negative thoughts and redirect you to more positive energy.
- Dreams are frequently used to communicate messages.
- Sometimes you may trip, sneeze, drop something, or be startled by a loud noise. These are all ways your guides use to get your attention.
- Your intuition, sixth sense, or gut instinct are part of your internal compass and some of the main ways angels and guides communicate with you.
- Recurring birds, animals, or objects in nature may convey a message.*

---

*For more information on animal and nature symbolism, see *Animal Speak: The Spiritual and Magical Powers of Creatures Great and Small* or *Nature-Speak: Signs, Omens, and Messages in Nature,* both by Ted Andrews.

- Your first thoughts when you awaken during the night or in the morning are usually guidance from your spirit team.
- Numbers on a clock when you wake up suddenly or recurring numbers may be messages.*
- Answers randomly popping into your head from earlier questions are usually messages from your angels and spirit guides.
- Coincidences, serendipity, or synchronicity are often the work of your spirit team.
- Song lyrics spontaneously playing in your head may be messages from your angels and guides.
- Muscle testing, dowsing, or using a pendulum can provide direction from your spirit team.
- Sudden aha moments are often placed in your mind by your angels and spirit guides.
- The first instantaneous response to a question is usually directly from your spirit team. Trust it! Your second or third responses are frequently from your mind.
- Ringing in your ears or tingling in your body, when not caused by a medical condition, are often used by your angels and guides to let you know they are there.
- Recurring thoughts or repeated suggestions from different sources are most likely guidance from your spirit team.
- Automatic writing is another way to get answers from your team. Ask your question and write in longhand as fast as you can. Let your hand guide your writing, not your mind.
- Meditation or quieting your busy mind makes it easier to feel or sense guidance from angels and guides.

The more you understand how angels and guides communicate with you, the easier it is to follow their guidance. Once you start

---

*See *Angel Numbers 101* by Doreen Virtue.

raising awareness of your spirit team, you will notice their messages all around you. They will *always* respond to your requests. Be patient, since they will give you only what you need to know in each moment. Be sure to remember to thank them for their intercession.

GUIDANCE FROM YOUR MIND VS. GUIDANCE FROM YOUR ANGELS AND GUIDES

I am frequently asked how to distinguish guidance from your own mind versus that coming from your guides and angels. Your mind will tell you that you *have to, need to,* or *should do* something, whereas guidance from your angels and guides just *feels* right—it's an inner knowing. Your mind's directives are fear-based, while the angels and guides offer you suggestions based on love.

Throughout this initial process of connecting with your angels and guides it's important to remember that they work in conjunction with the soul's desires, not the intellect, which sometimes bases its decisions on reasoning. The angels and guides must *always* follow the directives and intentions of your soul, regardless of what your mind wishes. This can sometimes be frustrating when your mind wants something very badly. But your soul directs your team: *No, don't create that* or *You are not to assist with complete healing at this time.* The soul is a very powerful part of you. It's up to you to become fully aware of that part of you, because it's who you truly are—your essence.

Your mind is an extremely powerful tool and can be very useful if you train it to work in harmony with Divine Source. This is something I'll expand on later. At this stage I want you to be listening to your soul and your intuition more than to your rational mind. Your mind provides far too much static and interference because it is profoundly connected to the material and superficial demands of the world. It is much more important at this point to connect with the divine aspect of yourself. After all, your rational mind got you into whatever trouble of negativity you are now experiencing.

Kyle—A Brief Case Study

A client whom I will call Kyle had a situation that illustrates my point. Kyle was a brilliant young professor of literature at a top university. When he reluctantly came to me for a consultation he listened rather incredulously as I told him many of the same things I've explained here. As we spoke, I could see his face twist into a frown, while his eyebrows furrowed angrily. "It just doesn't make rational sense," he muttered.

"Let me ask you something," I replied. "Are you happy?"

"Of course I'm not happy!" he exploded. "If I was happy, do you think I would have even come here—talking nonsense about angels, no less?"

"Call it whatever you want," I replied, "but why not give it a shot?"

"Because it goes against everything I stand for. My colleagues would laugh at me. I teach for a living. My mind is the most important tool I have."

Kyle walked out of my office that day, his shoulders slumped in pain. I knew not to chase after him because he needed to find his own path. About a year later I ran into him at a coffee shop. He looked utterly changed. His hair was longer, the small paunch he had been cultivating had disappeared, and his eyes twinkled with a profound joy that certainly wasn't coming from his rational mind.

As soon as he saw me, he grabbed my arm. "Robbie," he said, "it's so good to see you. I've been thinking about you recently. After our meeting I spent months—and I mean *months*—struggling with the fact that my intellectual side would not let me open my heart to the angelic realm. I would sit in my office going over the logic of it all, having imaginary arguments with myself. And then one day I did just what you said: I gave it a shot. I just thought to heck with it, what I'm doing isn't working, and no amount of logic or rationalizing is going to change that."

"What happened?" I asked trying to contain my curiosity.

"Well," Kyle gave me a broad smile, "I opened myself up to the spiritual world. And it was like a dam bursting." His voice rose with excitement. "I haven't been the same since. I feel like I'm living for the first time. My mind has actually expanded. Now I'm in regular communication with my guardian angel, and it has made my life so much better. I don't know what I was so afraid of."

ENGAGING MORE OF YOUR TEAM

You learned in chapter 1 that there are many more spiritual forces available to you than your guardian angel. In fact, there is an unlimited number of angels and spirit guides accessible to you. Engaging their support is the same process as with your guardian angel. Talk to them in your mind. Like your guardian angel, they are telepathic to your thoughts. As you explore more about different types of angels, archangels, Ascended Masters, and spirit guides, you can contact them for many different kinds of individual requests.

Matthew—A Brief Case Study

Another client whom I will call Matthew had long been in touch with his guardian angel but hadn't reached out to any of his other guides. He didn't feel as though he needed to. Things were going well in his life. He was happily married with a young son he doted on. Then one day he came home to the worst news a parent can receive: his son had been diagnosed with a difficult type of pediatric cancer.

As Matthew told me:

Seeing my boy in the hospital bed wrecked me. It was a pain so profound it is difficult to describe. He was a total innocent, and there were tubes running in and out of him. And medications and treatments were making him feel awful. Seeing that helpless little guy almost made me lose my faith in God, in myself, in even the possibility of there being divine forces watching over my family.

But instead of giving in to despair, I sent up a plea to the universe. I knew my guardian angel had my back, but I wanted to engage a full team of angels to help little MJ, who was only four. I committed all my energy to calling on a diverse team of celestial beings that would become the overseers of my son's recovery. I engaged Archangel Zaphiel, the protector of children, and every day I implored him to watch over and heal MJ. I engaged Archangel Raphael for his powerful tools of healing. I set up a shrine in my bedroom and lit candles and said prayers every night.

Miraculously, after a few months my son's cancer went into remission. The doctors couldn't believe it. They had only given him a 20 percent chance of survival for a year. But despite that dark projection, he made it. Yesterday, he and I played hide-and-seek, and to see him up and running around with such zest filled my heart with gratitude. Anything is possible when you have the power of the angelic realm at your fingertips.

Because this is a free-will planet, angels and spirit guides will not respond to your pleas to affect others. The exception is when you ask for help with your child who is not yet an adult. Upon your request, the angels and spirit guides will assist your young child in accordance with their soul's desires.

Now that you've read Matthew's story of angelic support, you are ready for the next step: namely, to determine which tools and techniques you will need, and how to use them to deepen your relationship with the many celestial beings and spirit guides waiting to assist you. I believe you will find what you need in the following chapter, and in the remainder of the book.

3

Tools of the Soul

The expectations of life depend upon diligence; the mechanic that would perfect his work must first sharpen his tools.

CONFUCIUS

Look inside your soul and find your tools. We all have tools and we have to live with the help of them.

RUTH GRUBER

DEVELOPING A CLOSER CONNECTION TO YOUR ANGELS AND GUIDES

An angelic relationship is like any other: it requires involvement, effort, and communication. If you are not taking enough time to foster your connection to your guides, your level of engagement with them will undoubtedly suffer. It helps to think of your relationship with your angels as similar to what you have with your best friend; if you don't call him or her for several months or don't return phone messages, it can put a strain on your friendship. The same is true for your relationship with your angels. If you cultivate your connection with your guides as you would your best friend, the bond will strengthen. And if you put sufficient energy into connecting with your guides, you will see many positive results in your daily life, as your investment in time will pay major dividends that will expand your spiritual, emotional, and personal growth.

⌒ Intention

Intention is an important catalyst for you to get closer to your angels and guides. You need to spend quality time with your spirit team to get to know them. Trust me, they will respond to your earnest desire to develop a closer bond. Try to put aside any preconceived beliefs or expectations on how that's going to happen. They communicate to you through your intuitive muscle, which may be weak and out of practice. Intuition takes time to grow, especially when it's been latent for a long time.

Employ your intention when calling forth your guardian angel and your guides; ask that they be with you in a more conscious way. Pay attention to the energy developing within you. Then validate what you're experiencing. Thank them for their presence. Once you leave the environment you have created with your angels and guides and go back to your day-to-day life, where you're bombarded by multiple energies, those feelings will begin to dissipate. So you need discipline to stay centered and to pay attention to your interaction with your spirit team. Be mindful of your intuitive feelings. Be patient, with them and with yourself. In time, the bond will get strong, but as with all relationships, this does not happen right away.

⌒ Journaling

Keeping a journal can sometimes be helpful. You might write something like, "I felt close to an energy that was very light-filled. I felt loved." As you continue to write, you might discover that you suddenly have ideas or thoughts that you've never had before. After you write everything down, please don't just put it in a drawer and forget about it. Read your entries regularly. Journaling reinforces the experience of connecting with your spirit team and confirms that things in your life are changing.

Be patient with this process. Everyone has a different level of connection to the higher-frequency dimensions. Yours may take more time to develop than some others. Don't become discouraged. Always remember that you are part of Divine Source and trust the process. Now you're in the process of accessing it, which signals a very exciting transformation in your life.

DEEPEN YOUR CONNECTION WITH YOUR ANGEL AND SPIRIT GUIDES

I have found the following practices useful in my personal journey, and my clients have consistently reported positive results using these practices over the years.

⌒ Create a Shrine

It's helpful to have a dedicated place in your home where you can build a shrine. This shrine is a sacred place that serves as your spiritual center. Over time, this designated area will become filled with sacred energy that will make it easier to connect to the higher frequencies of your guides and angels.

Once you have selected a quiet place for your shrine, add whatever items call to you. Be creative and choose items that have personal significance. These may include:

- Fresh flowers: Roses have the highest frequency of all flowers. White flowers are preferable to color-processed flowers or commercial floral arrangements.

- Candles: Unscented white candles are best.
- Bells, chimes, or drums
- Crystals
- Pictures or statues of spiritual figures and angels
- Photos of ancestors

It's important to meditate for a minimum of five to fifteen minutes in this space each day. It's better to do a few minutes daily in this same location rather than an hour once a week. You want to steadily build the energy around your shrine. This is important. Envision this space as a place to connect with your guides and angels and make it a part of your daily spiritual practice.

⌒ Meditation to Connect to Your Angels and Guides

Get into a comfortable seated position. Close your eyes and take three deep breaths, inhaling and exhaling slowly, relaxing a little more with each breath.

In your mind, create a safe environment. Envision an inviting place where you will meet with your angels or guides. You could be going through a garden gate, down a flower-lined path, across a meadow, or sitting on a bench next to a waterfall. Or you might see yourself seated in a rocking chair next to a crackling fireplace, with an empty chair across from you where your angel or spirit guide will join you. If you prefer the seaside, you may imagine yourself walking along a deserted beach as warm, foamy waves wash over your feet as they sink into the damp sand.

When you are mentally serene and comfortable, either sitting still or walking slowly, mentally call to your angels or guides, inviting them to join you. Imagine they are next to you, hearing your every thought. Ask them any questions you like. It's unlikely you will get a response to your questions in that moment, but in the days and weeks that follow you will likely receive subtle answers to some of those questions.

When you have finished a dialogue with your angels or guides, thank them for joining you. Walk back down the path you came from, closing the gate behind you—actually or figuratively. Have the intention to end the meditation. Return back into the energy of Earth by imagining tree roots sprouting from the soles of your feet and growing down to the center of the Earth. After a minute or two, bring your focus back to your breath. Take three slow, deep breaths and gradually open your eyes.

⌒ Strengthening Your Intuition

Intuition is one of the most powerful tools available to each of us. Sometimes referred to as your inner guidance, sixth sense, or gut instinct, your intuition is a means of deep knowing and certainty that is not based on reasoning or thinking things through. Intuition is how your subconscious mind communicates information to your conscious mind. That's why it's such a remarkable and reliable source of inner wisdom.

In the past, we humans were much better at using our intuition. In today's hectic, noisy world where we are bombarded by information around the clock, most people are too busy to quiet their talkative mind and listen to their subtle internal GPS, or direction finder. Unfortunately, when we stop this kind of soul-deep listening and lose touch with our inner guidance, we frequently run into trouble.

Your intuition is designed to help you navigate life more easily. Whether you want to make the best possible decisions or resolve problems quickly, achieving your goals faster and more successfully happens when you combine your logical thought process with your intuition. It's a key ingredient in the recipe for a more joyful and satisfying existence.

Intuition is a tool that everyone has, though to different degrees. Your intuition might speak to you as a flash of insight, a hunch, or an idea. Your intuition may also be perceived physically, such as a feeling of relief throughout your body, goose bumps, or discomfort in your stomach. Intuitive messages may come through your emotions. You may feel apprehension or distrust when you're being guided toward or away from something or someone. When you're following your intuition, your life will flow more easily, allowing you to feel happier and more peaceful. It's a difficult step for many people to take, but letting go of the rational process we have all been trained to cling to and letting one's intuition take over is very freeing.

The key mechanism of this transition is to be able to tap into what's going on inside of you. Like developing a muscle, the more you use your intuition, the stronger it gets. Below you'll find some suggestions on how to strengthen your intuitive process:

Meditate. Regular meditation can be incredibly effective. To develop your intuition, quiet your busy mind and listen to your inner wisdom for a minimum of ten minutes throughout the day. As you do this, you will notice thoughts arising. It is a matter of *when* thoughts will appear, not *if*. Even advanced meditators experience the busy mind (it's only natural). Beginning meditators tend to get discouraged and give up, criticizing themselves for not being able to stop their mind. The remedy is to be aware of the ebb and flow of thoughts and *not follow them*, but continue to relax the mind, perhaps seeing them as bubbles rising and disappearing.

Take time to be alone. Meditation is more challenging for some people than for others. If you aren't able to meditate, take a few minutes to separate yourself from other people. Have the intention to engage your intuition. Clear your mind of distractions and turn your attention inward. Then try not to think—just let go and feel. Your mind is constantly thinking and is always chattering away. Your mind often argues with your intuition rather than following it. Your intuition, on the other hand, *feels*. To distinguish whether a thought is coming from your mind or your intuition, try to differentiate whether you're thinking or feeling. Be patient, because it takes practice to make this distinction.

Listen to your body. Your body is an excellent conduit for your intuition. When you have decisions to make, pay attention to your gut feeling. If you have an uncomfortable physical sensation about something, don't ignore it. Your body doesn't lie. It will tell you when you aren't with the appropriate person, in the proper place, or making the best choice.

Journal. This is an effective way to receive information and guidance from a higher consciousness. It's a good idea to journal for a minimum of five to ten minutes each day. Use stream-of-consciousness or automatic writing to gain insights about areas where you want more clarity.

Do heart exercises. Sit in a comfortable position. Think of something you love to do or a place that you enjoy. Allow what you identified to settle into your heart. Imagine your heart is breathing now, instead of your lungs. Focus your love on that enjoyable thing or place in your heart for three to five minutes. Use your intuition to sense if there is insight about the nurtured thing or place in your heart. For example, if you love the sea, picture yourself on a deserted beach with the gulls wheeling overhead and the sound of the surf ringing in your ears. Envision this scene until you can allow yourself to sink into it and sense its reality.

The more you practice using your intuition, the stronger your intuition becomes. As you strengthen your intuitive muscle, you'll gain more confidence and trust your intuition, making it much easier to accept that your extra sense that connects you to the higher dimensions is sending you an important message.

USING YOUR MIND AS A
POWERFUL TOOL

Your mind is an incredibly powerful tool—but it is exactly that, a tool. More specifically, your mind is a *servant* to the soul. Always remember that the soul is in control. Your mind wants to be involved and in control of *everything.* Your mind reflects your ego. But your mind was never supposed to be running the show. Your soul is intended to be in charge of your life—with your mind as a supporting player.

We often get into trouble by asking our mind to make decisions it was never intended to make. Your soul is a higher consciousness and knows the best way to accomplish its goals. Your mind is intended to support the soul, not resist it. While your mind may be good at balancing a checkbook, it does not know how to find the most satisfying and fulfilling job. Your soul knows which career is best in this incarnation for what it wants you to experience and master. Your mind doesn't know how to find the best long-term romantic relationship for you. Your mind doesn't know how to be the best parent, partner, teacher, or lover. All of these deep decisions should be governed by your heart and soul.

Our world today provides a good example of what happens when our minds are in control. The result is negativity, fear, greed, and war. When you follow the dictates of your mind, you can get into trouble and create more pain and struggle than your soul ever intended.

However, learning how to control your mind and your thoughts is a lifelong journey, which accounts for the growing popularity of meditation. Meditation trains the mind to be still, even if only for a few seconds at a time. Meditation briefly pushes the pause button of our thoughts. Once a client told me she felt like her mind was like a two-year-old let loose with a chainsaw. When you clear and learn to control your thoughts, suddenly you can get the two-year-old to put the chainsaw down, pause, and allow your higher intuitive self to ask, *Is this what I really want to be thinking?*

Meditation teaches you how to quiet this noisy chatter just enough so that you can move more consciously toward love-based thoughts over fear-based ones, and mindfully focus on a new and more positive direction for your life. One of the biggest benefits of quieting your mind through mediation is that it more easily allows you to feel the inner wisdom of your soul, guides, and angels. When you succeed in doing this you become an incredibly powerful creator and self-healer.

Instead of focusing on depressing thoughts, begin to think about what you're grateful for. Instead of thinking about lack or not having enough money, think about the abundance you do have in your life—people who love you, healthy children, your health, a sense of humor, etc. Don't think about what went wrong on a particular day; think of the dozens of things that went right. To be clear, I am not advocating a head-in-the-sand approach. What I am suggesting is that you focus on what you *want* and not what you don't want or don't have. This important change in your thinking will undoubtedly attract more of what you want into your life.

Make no mistake, our minds are incredibly powerful! Where your attention goes, energy flows, and that's what you ultimately create. Become conscious of what you're thinking about most of the time. Is what you're obsessing about really what you want to create in your life?

When you *intentionally* use your powerful mind, with your angels and guides on your team, you can do amazing things. Using your angels and spirit guides in conjunction with your mind is like taking your potential from 5 amps of power to 5,000 amps of power in an instant. Now you're cooking! That's what was always intended—to *mindfully* and *intentionally* create with your powerful mind while using assistance from the other side of the veil. Do you see the big picture now, and how this synchronicity is designed to work?

At this point you might be wondering exactly how to achieve this mind-soul balance. I like the image of putting a higher consciousness behind the wheel of the car instead of your mind. That higher consciousness can be your soul, your angels, your benevolent spirit guides, or Divine Source. You then allow it to steer the car toward your greater goals. You will soon realize that you will reach your destination in a wonderful and exacting way, because a higher consciousness was always intended to be in the driver's seat.

Whenever you engage the services of your angels and guides, your mind has to let go of two burning questions: *How?* and *When?* The mind is a control freak and wants all the *i*'s dotted and the *t*'s crossed. When you hand things over to your spirit team, your mind will tend to be like a small child who continually asks, "How are we going to get there? When are we going to get there? Are we there yet?" You've got to let those types of questions go, and instead stay curious and excited.

While your angels and guides are taking you on this journey to get you what you've asked for—or, more accurately, *the real need behind what you've asked for*—always keep your mind focused on the end result. In your mind's eye see yourself having already achieved your goal. What does that feel like? Maybe you feel incredibly grateful. Using all your senses, add details of what it looks and feels like to have reached your objective—the more emotion you can summon, the better. Stay focused on your goal but be open to alternative results.

Your spirit team is governed and limited by Natural Laws and Spiritual Laws. They will *always* respond to every single request, but do so according the highest good of all and your soul's intentions. Your guides and angels work within the parameters of your soul's desires. Let's say you're hoping a romance with a coworker will work out. Please know that your angels and guides will *not* help you with this romance if it is unsuitable, but they understand the deep desire you have for love, so they will bring you a romantic relationship with someone your soul believes is better suited for you. It's important to remember that your soul knows your higher good and always serves that higher good—even if you yourself cannot see it as such.

TRUSTING YOUR INNER GPS

When it comes to interacting with angels and spirit guides, you're going to need to pay attention to your body. Every person is *clairsentient,* meaning they can feel or sense guidance within their body, particularly in the solar plexus area. Very few people are *clairaudient,* meaning they hear their angels and guides, or *clairvoyant,* meaning they see them. You should not expect to hear or see your angels and guides when you try to connect to them. Over time, however, you will be able to *feel* their guidance in your heart and in the pit of your stomach.

Your guides and angels respond to every request you send them. Helping you is extremely easy for them, and it is their tremendous joy. Do not worry about angels connecting with you. If they need to get a message to you, they will—one way or another. As one of my spirit guides told me, *If we need to make a movie or write a book to get our message across, we will. Whatever it takes, we will find a way to get our messages and guidance across to you.*

If you miss their messages, they'll continue to send them to you. They may use different tactics or sources. Personally, the second or third time I've gotten the same guidance from different sources, I pay attention. Don't worry—you'll pick up on their guidance eventually. They are very good at what they do. It is as easy as child's play for them. It is a key part of the universal design that you pick up on this important guidance.

If you truly feel you aren't getting *any* messages, it's possible you are in a holding pattern and there is divine timing involved. Perhaps there are no messages for you at the moment, or you're on a need-to-know basis. If it's essential that you need to know something, they'll make sure you get it. Just relax and trust in yourself and your spirit team.

Over time you'll grow more adept at reading the mostly nonverbal signs and messages that angels and guides send you. In the beginning, recognizing these signs can be a challenge, especially when we're bogged down in daily activities. It's not uncommon for people to tell me they just aren't seeing the signs their spirit guides and angels are giving them. Sometimes, as happened with a client of mine named Sean, we miss the signs or misunderstand how our guides are helping us. A few months after working with me, Sean wrote me a distraught email, complaining that he wasn't receiving clear signals from his team.

Sean—A Brief Case Study

Dear Robbie:

I've been communicating with my angels for three months. I pray and talk to them about my wishes every day. I ask them to help me. How do I know that they will grant my wishes? They're so quiet and peaceful. I asked them to respond to me and give me some signs, but so far I have received none. When I meditate, I ask them to reveal themselves in my dreams, but they do not appear. When I talk to them, I feel nothing, not even a sensation of warmth. Are my wishes impossible? Are they too much? Do I not deserve their help? I'm confused and lost. Please kindly respond with your advice on what to do.

Sean

My reply:

Dear Sean:

Your angels assure me that they hear you. They always respond to every single request, but they do so according to the highest and best good of all, which they see far more clearly than you do. They also respond according to your soul's intentions. Your soul does not intend for you to have exactly what you have asked for. However, the angels are in the process of bringing you something else that will take its place. This has nothing to do with you "deserving" what you asked for or that what you requested is "too much." What you are to experience in this lifetime must be aligned with your soul's desires.

Again, your angels do hear you and they are responding. But they are not reacting in the way your mind expects them to. Even though you have asked for it, it is uncommon to receive an immediate response in your meditations or in your dreams. Release any expectations of how they will communicate with or help you. They will respond in the way and time that is appropriate—and in your best interests.

Like most people, you are clairsentient only, which means that you feel their guidance. You will not see or hear your angels and guides. Because of the way you are wired in this lifetime, you will not feel a sensation of warmth. I do not feel that either.

Connecting with your angelic team is like learning a new language, skill, or sport. It's a process that requires practice and patience. Ask your angels to help you improve your ability to recognize and understand their guidance and signs. You can also ask them to help you improve your intuition, develop more trust, and help you enhance your ability to communicate with them.

You will get there, Sean. It requires patience, but allowing your angels to help you is a very worthwhile pursuit. Your angels are responding to you in the way they are permitted to respond. Be persistent. Your angels love you more deeply than you can possibly imagine.

Love,

Robbie

I am sharing Sean's email and my response to illustrate how often we may be helped but we don't even know it. To combat this sense of "unknowing" and open your eyes, I'll highlight some common ways angels and guides communicate and provide help. Many of these examples come from my own life.

I'm not triggered. Assistance from angels and spirit guides comes in many forms. When you're getting help, triggers are softened and you unhook from them easier. You don't go down the rabbit hole of fearful, negative thoughts as often. Many years ago, a lifelong friend of mine had become increasingly critical of her coworkers. In our phone chats she often complained that she had to compensate for them not pulling their weight, which burdened her with extra work. After several months of listening to her complaints, I began to resent how negative our conversations had become, so I began avoiding her calls. At one point I decided to ask my angels and spirit guides to help me heal the relationship with my friend. Immediately, I felt a strong wave of compassion for her move through my body. The next time my friend called, instead of feeling annoyed by her complaining I stopped judging her behavior and felt a calm acceptance of her situation. Interestingly, my new nonjudgmental attitude made it possible for me to be objective. With that objectivity I was able to give her some measured advice and strategies for dealing with the state of affairs—which she took to heart. Thankfully it all turned out for the best and, of course, I heartily thanked my angels and spirit guides for helping me feel compassion for my friend.

Random thoughts suddenly come to me. Angels love assisting you with simple things. They know it's the little things each day that make a difference, and they are always there to assist us. I remember once, just as I was running out the door for a meeting, the thought popped into my head, out of nowhere, to grab my forgotten briefcase. Some people have Siri on their smartphones or tablets. That helpful voice in my head was my "celestial Siri."

Let go. Your spirit guides lovingly encourage you to let go of everything that doesn't serve you. When I was younger, the needs of my family and demanding career often left me stressed and physically exhausted. I felt guilty taking time for myself. My health continued to deteriorate as I held on to the belief that my needs weren't as worthy of attention. Eventually I asked myself how bad does it have to get before I let go of this unhealthy lifestyle? Then I asked my angels and spirit guides to help me take better care of myself. Almost immediately my packed schedule began to open up. I found myself actually wanting to nurture myself. As a result, my life became much more balanced and less stressful.

Things aren't flowing. Your mind doesn't know the best ways to heal your illness, find a fulfilling job, or attract an ideal romantic partner. Your mind is designed to intuitively follow guidance from a higher consciousness on how best to do these things. When your mind takes over and ignores the guidance coming from a higher consciousness, you are most likely going to find yourself faced with continual obstacles. Some years ago when I was searching for a house, I found what I *thought* was the perfect place. However, every time I tried to contact the seller something kept us from connecting. Initially she was unable to be contacted because she was traveling overseas. When she returned to the States, her phone wasn't working. For the next few days, I followed my intuition. This led me to a newly listed house with a wonderful yard that I absolutely loved. Because of the barriers of connecting with the owner of the first house, I ended up with a better home with a beautiful yard. I now realize that the obstacles were the way my angels and spirit guides led me to a better-suited home. Bottom line: When you're following your soul's guidance, it feels right, requires less effort, and isn't forced. Opportunities open up. Things fall into place. An ideal office setting becomes available to you. Clients who need your services find you. When you get in the supportive flow, you enjoy what you're doing and feel fulfilled.

Synchronicities happen. It's easy for your spirit team to create synchronicities. A serendipitous event is a sign that they are deliberately bringing something to you. If within a short time two people suggest reading the same book, you're likely being divinely guided toward that particular book. Synchronicities are a validation that your spirit team is working in your behalf.

Consciousness increases. Like breadcrumbs gradually leading you down the path to your desired goal, you may get little bits and pieces of information that may seem disconnected. But then a friend or coworker may say something that sparks an aha moment for you. Or one morning you have an insight the moment you wake up. As more pieces are revealed, your awareness of the bigger picture increases. One day you suddenly realize that even a negative event, such as when you suffered a broken ankle, for example, allowed you to become more compassionate toward people with disabilities. Your enlightenment now generates more loving responses to other people's challenges.

TRUST YOUR INSTINCTS

The final tool I want you to remember to always keep handy is the most basic and also one of the most powerful: *instinct*. I sometimes define instinct as the opposite of fear. Your spirit guides and angels will not guide you through your fears. Rather, with great love they will guide you through your instincts. When you're faced with a decision in a specific moment, a three-second gut check is enough to tell you whether it feels right. You will have a "knowing" as to whether or not this is the next step to take. If you pause longer than three seconds to discern the answer, your mind is now actively involved—which can negate the power of your initial instinct.

If you are doing something because you feel you "should," or you "have to," or you'd feel guilty if you didn't do it, you have allowed your fear-based mind to override your divinely inspired instincts. A fail-safe tip to determine whether guidance is (ideally) coming from a higher consciousness or from your rational mind is to ask yourself: *Is this coming from a place of love or fear?*

Here is my best and most important advice on every decision you make in life, whether personal or professional: always operate from a place of love, never fear or anger or hatred. If you take nothing else away from this book, I implore you to remember this. Once you are living a love-based existence, your intuition will become incredibly powerful. Your instincts and your spirit team will function as one seamless unit, masterfully guiding you through this existence that we call life.

⦿

4

Turning Struggles
into Successes

The battles that count aren't the ones for gold medals.
The struggles within yourself—the invisible, inevitable
battles inside all of us—that's where it's at.

JESSE OWENS

The first three chapters of this book are an introductory gateway for your communication with higher-frequency beings on the other side of the veil. Hopefully, once you acknowledge your spirit team and accept yourself as comprised of Divine Source, then you will know that their assistance is always available to you.

Now you will learn better how to contact angels and guides, recognize their communication methods, and continue to deepen your connection with them. Then you can apply this knowledge to the practical matters of your daily life. It is time to learn about the many issues that angels and guides can help you with and also learn how their assistance can be useful in situations you are dealing with. And we are all dealing with such situations every day.

This is the first of four chapters dealing with the particular problems with which angels are frequently called on to help. The following chapters will show you, directly and clearly, how their love and guidance can fundamentally alter the way you approach your challenges, whether big or small, and thus how your spirit team can change your life dramatically.

Let's start with the basic things that concern us most: love, money, professional fulfillment, and accomplishing the many goals we set out for ourselves. Angels can, in fact, play a key role in supporting and guiding you in matters involving career development and financial stability, among other basic aspects of your life.

The four sections of this chapter will illuminate how celestial guides help with financial matters, including obtaining a fulfilling job and finding your personal power at work. It's extremely useful to engage help from angels and guides for many of your professional goals, including being assertive, fulfilling responsibilities, and seizing your personal power.

We conclude with a reminder that angels always respond to every single request from you. It is crucial to remember that while angels and guides always answer every request, they do so only *in accord with the highest and best good for all,* and in harmony with your soul's intentions. For instance, you may want a luxury car, but your soul may be seeking something far more meaningful. You can count on your angels to always act for your highest good, even though you might not be aware of what that highest good might be.

MAKING SENSE OF YOUR MONEY

When it comes to assisting with financial issues, angels use a wide spectrum of methods to come to our aid. Angels have no use for money but they understand that our world is governed by currency in a significant way, and that your financial situation can be either a conduit or a roadblock to your security. The angels' intent is to eliminate any obstacles that impede your climb toward spiritual enlightenment and personal happiness.

People are frequently surprised that angels want to help humans with financial concerns. They seem skeptical as to why angels would have a true desire to assist with matters as mundane as rent, bills, or tuition. Angels do not attribute any power to money. They recognize that money is simply a tool. Their intent is to free us of the everyday concerns that weigh us down, especially regarding money, which many view as a prime obstacle to peace of mind.

Unlike creditors, banks, salespeople, or even some investment planners, angels have no ulterior motive or agenda when it comes to money. Greed would be as foreign to an angel as algebra would be to an alligator—it simply isn't in their ken. Just think how incredible that is—you have an entire team of beings who will guide you through financial chaos totally free of charge, totally free of sinister motives.

When you ask for angelic help with financial concerns, your team immediately goes into action in your behalf. Their methods are custom-tailored to each situation. Angels often take a surprising approach, opening avenues and opportunities you had not considered previously. At first this might seem like a vague concept, but in time you'll realize how endlessly useful it can be. Angels expertly guide us toward solutions you had not thought of, attuning us to new possibilities, because our previous rational mindset had gotten in the way of a greater, more cosmic understanding.

But first and most importantly, you must ask for help. By asking to have your financial needs met, you allow many new possibilities for successful outcomes to become available to you. But you cannot receive help until you ask first. For instance, a client of mine named

Elayna was wondering how she was going to pay her daughter's college tuition.

Elayna—A Brief Case Study (Part 1)
This is what Elayna told me:

> I had been divorced from my husband for three years, and I was still holding a great deal of anger toward him. He had basically left my daughter and me high and dry when she was about fifteen and did the least he could for her. Now that she was technically an adult, he wasn't liable for any more child support payments, and the checks stopped arriving in the mail. What a guy, right?
>
> At this same time, my daughter, who is the light of my life, was admitted to a prestigious but very expensive college. She was thrilled and so was I, but I'm only a receptionist at a doctor's office. It has always been my dream for my daughter to achieve higher goals than I have, but when I saw the cost of college tuition I knew that my salary wasn't going to cover it. I began to panic, not knowing where the money was going to come from, filled with fear that I was going to let my only daughter down. I was overwhelmed by the problem, which seemed to have no solution, and I felt like I was at the end of my rope. She'd applied for financial aid, but it didn't begin to cover the costs. There didn't seem to be any good options.

In today's world, with high divorce rates and exorbitant tuitions, Elayna's problem is a common one. Thankfully, it is not one that is out of the reach of an angelic team. In response to Elayna's fears, I gave her the following advice:

Ask for what you need. Ask your spirit team to help you. Loosen your fearful mind's controlling grip on the *how* and *when* the tuition problem will be resolved. Trust that it *will happen* if it is the intention of your daughter's soul to go to college, including this particular one.

Focus on what you want. Don't focus on your doubts or obstacles. That only energizes them. Redirect your mind so that it's focused on the solutions to the tuition dilemma and reasons how and why this will happen. Don't focus on the reasons it won't work.

Feel gratitude daily. Be grateful every day for all the abundance and many blessings in your life. You can express your gratitude in many ways, by making lists, either verbal or written, of the things you are grateful for. Journaling is also very helpful.

Let it go. If you slip into fear or doubt about the tuition issue, take a deep breath and use three powerful words: *Let it go.* Don't let your fearful mind drag you into the past or the future. Stay present. Find reassurance in thinking, *My angels are working on this.* Keep repeating this until the doubt disappears.

Listen for guidance. Be quiet for a few minutes each day to intuitively feel your team's guidance on ways to manifest the needed college funds. If your mind insists there's no time, find peaceful respites throughout the day to quiet your busy mind.

Act on their advice. Take inspired or directed action from your spirit team. They may guide you through what seems like a sudden hunch, or a coincidence may happen. Synchronistic signs might lead you to apply for a particular scholarship or take another specific action. Pay attention to their guidance and act on it.

Keep handing it over. If you feel overwhelmed about obtaining college funds, remind yourself that you and your brain don't have to figure it out. You've assigned the task of paying for tuition to your angels and guides, so relax and trust.

Visualize that it is accomplished. Visualizations that are filled with vivid, sensory details can be effective. Imagine the pride you will feel after all the tuition has been paid and your daughter graduates. In your imagination see her walking across the stage to receive her diploma.

When Elayna realized she had an angelic hand guiding her, solutions opened up that previously seemed impossible. She felt her team guide her to a women's center, where they helped her apply for scholarships that were only available to the children of single mothers. Now her daughter is in her second year of college, earning straight A's without accruing massive amounts of student debt. Some day when she's a big success she'll pay it forward to someone else. Isn't it incredible how angels work?

Elayna's story can act as a powerful template for your own actions. From now on, whenever you have a financial problem, challenge, or dilemma, present it to your personal spirit team: your guardian angel and your celestial board of advisors. Once you do that, they will work in your behalf. Then sit back and wait for guidance. You must learn to release the worry and concern. Keep asking for help until your matter is resolved.

FINDING A FULFILLING JOB

Searching for a job, especially in today's tough economy, can be emotionally exhausting and lead to a false sense of failure because there can be many disappointments along the way. The constant struggle and the unrewarded effort can spiral into paralyzing fear and fill you with self-doubt. It doesn't help when you go on social media and find pictures of friends and acquaintances smiling, surrounded by happy coworkers, or holding some award bestowed on them. It can seem overwhelming, leading you to believe that everyone else is tapped into some beautiful, shiny reality you are locked out of.

Even if you are gainfully employed it may not be the job or career of your dreams. That could mean you are stuck at a low-level job while you dream of being a high-powered executive. Or you *are* a high-powered executive who dreams of being able to do something more creative and independent. The point is that if your work is not attuned to your soul's intentions, you undoubtedly will feel unfulfilled.

Dustin—A Brief Case Study

One such example was a young man named Dustin. He wasn't a client of mine. Dustin was the son of a longtime friend. He was a bright kid, interested in music and the arts, with a real knack for songwriting. Like some creative young people, he also had a tendency to depression, and so he self-medicated with marijuana and alcohol. Over the years I saw the circles under his eyes darken, his shoulders begin to slump, and his voice grow listless. His interest in music and other artistic endeavors waned. By his late twenties he still hadn't made any progress in his career, bouncing around in a series of retail jobs he hated and pizza delivery gigs he took because he could smoke weed during work hours. In short, he'd become a burnout.

One day Dustin came to see me, telling me he was frustrated and ready to give up on his dream of working in the music industry. I told him I believed I had a way for him to fulfill his dream. I explained that he had tremendous help available to him that he wasn't using. I described how everyone on the planet, regardless of their belief system, always has help available from their guardian angel, and that we are meant to take advantage of their loving assistance.

I also explained that these benevolent beings are there to help us but need to be invited before they are able to step in and make a difference. I told Dustin that once they are called on for their help, they respond every single time and act according to our soul's intentions. I also told him that I believed it was his soul's desire for him to work in the music industry.

His lower lip trembled as he said emphatically, "I've had this passion for music ever since I was a little kid. I don't want to give up on it, but I don't know how to make it happen. I can't figure it out."

I smiled and leaned forward. "Maybe that's the problem—you're trying to figure it out with your mind. The mind isn't designed to know how to create the best job for you, or even what the best career might be. The mind is designed to intuitively follow your soul's guidance on what job and career would be perfect for you. Your soul knows what goals and lessons it wants to accomplish in this lifetime—and how best to achieve them."

I added, "Our minds are very powerful tools. Your mind is designed to serve your soul. Despite the value on intellect that we hold in esteem in this culture, the mind is not supposed to be in charge. Today's world currently reflects what happens when the mind is in charge. And that is scary."

Dustin was listening with interest as I continued. "It's always been the intent for the mind to follow guidance from the soul—which is a higher consciousness. The best way to achieve your goal—any goal— is to hand it over to a higher consciousness and intuitively follow the guidance. That higher consciousness can be Divine Source, your soul, your higher self, or an Ascended Master, guardian angel, or benevolent spirit guide. Because they hold a higher level of consciousness than your mind does, they know what's best for you and how to achieve it."

Dustin shook his head. "Wait a minute, wait a minute. I know my mind and it is *not* going to relinquish control. I'm a very logical guy. I don't believe in wishful thinking."

"It's a lot easier than you think," I replied. "Don't let your mind tell you otherwise."

"Alright. I'm not entirely convinced of all this, but I'll give it a try," he said. "I'll ask my guardian angel to help guide me to the best job."

"When you go where your soul intends, you're going to love your destination. I can't wait to see where your angels take you." I smiled brightly.

Several months later, Dustin called to give me an update on his life:

I was doing my usual routine. I'd wake up, take a toke, and dress for work at the pizza shop. But one morning I felt this strong urge to send a few of my recent recordings to a dozen music production houses. As soon as I got home from work, I looked online at the long list of music production companies. I got a sense as to which companies I should submit my work. They just felt right, y'know?

A few weeks later, a local music production house contacted me. They were impressed enough to give me a trial run, so they hired me. I now love my job and being around other people who share my passion. I did really well and before long I became an assistant track producer. It's not like I'm a rock star or anything, but I've finally found something that's fulfilling and has a future.

That's what I think I was always lacking in my life: the possibility of a future that mattered to me. Now that I have that, I wake up with energy that is the polar opposite of the burned-out feeling that pulled me down. I can't tell you how grateful I am to be free of that unwanted weight, and I do know it was more than just me that instigated the change. It feels great to actually look forward to something that excites me every single day.

Dustin's story offers lessons that can apply to anyone's situation. If you are unhappy in your current employment situation, ask your angelic team for help, and they will undoubtedly respond. Don't be afraid to pursue actions based on your hunches, and allow yourself to believe in the power and importance of what people call *coincidence*. This is just code for angelic help.

I would strongly urge you to follow the suggestions and guidance of your guides and angels. When in doubt, take the plunge. People never wish they had stayed in a bad situation longer—they always wonder why they hadn't gotten out sooner. Let your angels and guides help you find the job, career, or passion you deserve, the one that will lead you to a fulfilling life based on love, not one where you are mired in boredom or frustration. Just know that there is always a way out of a stalled work situation if you listen to your spirit team and let them take the reins.

FINDING YOUR POWER

One common complaint I hear is that people are not in control of their professional lives. They feel like they are being taken advantage of financially, are afraid to ask for a promotion, feel belittled or talked-down-to, or are simply not being given enough opportunities to show their skills and talents. *Languishing* is a word I often hear, even from those in their so-called ideal jobs.

The fact is, especially in professional or high-stakes situations, we often let ourselves be governed by fear-based thinking. Fear robs us of our ability to think straight and seize the moment when we need to the most. Fear is a default emotion that tangles our thinking.

Liz—A Brief Case Study
Another client, a twenty-six-year-old woman named Liz, was employing this kind of fear-based thinking when she was in a difficult work situation. It was something that no one should be subjected to but that many are. As she explained,

I moved to Manhattan for a job I had always wanted: a copy-writer at a successful advertising agency with some really good accounts. This was my big shot. Bright lights, large city, and ample paycheck! After only a few weeks on the job, I realized that my direct supervisor had a real Napoleon complex. He would strut around the office like a preening rooster, always override me in meetings, and take credit for my work. He would criticize me and my work at social situations such as after-hours company parties while placing himself in a posi-tion of unwarranted power, making me feel unfairly judged and even doubting my own abilities.

One day he even came on to me in a most sexual and dis-gusting way, putting his hand on my rear end as I got some-thing out of a drawer, muttering something I won't repeat. It was at that moment that I knew I had to find my power and take action.

Liz and I had worked together in the past, so she was accus-tomed to using her celestial team. In this particular situation she called on the help of Archangel Michael. I'll let her explain how it all worked out.

I knew Archangel Michael was a powerful celestial being, a supreme leader who had been helping people combat the forces of darkness for centuries. So the day after my boss put his hand where it should never have been I walked slowly toward his office, calling on Archangel Michael to guide me. I silently appealed to him: *Please Archangel Michael, I'm terrified and I need the power of your strength. Please give me the courage and honesty to do what I need to do and say what needs to be said.*

As I said these words to myself, I felt Michael's tremendous strength flow through me as I stood my ground and confronted my boss. I told him that what he had done was unacceptable and that I wanted to be immediately transferred to a different department. He squirmed in his chair and stammered but assured me the requested transfer would happen. And it did.

Now I have my own human team as well as my celestial one. We all treat one another with respect. I guess you could say my angels sure had an impact.

Liz had learned the lessons from her angels and was able to find her power with the support of Michael, an all-powerful archangel.

REQUESTS ARE FULFILLED ACCORDING TO YOUR SOUL'S INTENTIONS

A frequent, if misguided, complaint that I hear from my clients—especially when the subject is money—is this: "My guides aren't helping me. They're not giving me what I need and want, even when I ask for financial support."

The answer is simple: they are not giving you what your mind *thinks* it wants. They are leading you toward what your soul *knows* you need. Your soul has the wisdom of the many lifetimes in which it has existed in physical form. Consequently, your soul has a voice that is infinitely wiser than the voice of your mind, which has only existed for one lifetime. Often you're not even aware of that subtle, soul-level voice.

Your soul is your essence. It is the real you. If you are veering off in a direction that does not serve you on a soul level, your soul will put obstacles in your way. Those obstacles are purely a manifestation of a soul-deep self-correction. When you are moving in an unhealthy direction, the soul knows that and you will unconsciously create barriers.

For example, your mind insists that you need a brand-new Porsche and gives you a litany of reasons why you should go right out and buy one, even though you cannot afford it. Meantime, your soul whispers that you should be saving that money to buy a much-needed home for your family, or for some other practical purpose. In this disconnect between the part of your mind that is pure ego—wanting to make a splash in the world and look successful—and the you with a higher purpose, there is one thing you can be darn sure of: obtaining that Porsche is ultimately not going to be the thing you really need, and could become a burden.

This is one area where our angels come in handy, helping us when we're unwilling to listen to the whisperings of our soul. Be assured, however, that your guide or angel is not there to say, *You have to do this* or *You need to do that*. They will never issue directives or force you to do anything. Your soul is in charge, but your spirit team will help you hear it more clearly. As you practice centering and calling forth help from your angels and guides, you will develop in a way that allows you to more easily recognize the wisdom of your soul. For now, understand that your soul is always present and watchful. Pay attention to it. Do not ignore its wisdom in favor of the feeble protestations of your demanding and often childish ego mind that wants what it wants, when it wants it.

When your guardian angel and spirit team work on a cause in your behalf, profound possibilities open up. Your life will have more ease and greater joy and fulfillment than you can even imagine. If you follow the spiritual path, a positive outcome is inevitable—including where money matters are concerned. This has never failed a single person I've worked with, and I've been doing this for many years.

©©

5

Walking a Healing Path

The wound is the place where the Light enters you.

RUMI

❧

*P*ain is one of the most consequential and impactful forces in
the universe. It only takes an instant to enter our consciousness, yet a life can be forever altered in the blink of an eye. It can seem
like a cruel joke when we find ourselves spending years, or in some
cases even a lifetime, recovering from a single painful moment—for
example, the blinding flash of a car accident or an unexpected dis-
covery of infidelity. As anyone dealing with heartbreak or depression
knows, pain is not just a physical sensation; it can also be an ailment
of the mind. There are many types of pain. Some are deeper and
more profound than others. Relief from any of its manifestations can
seem like an impossible dream. But heal we must if we are to live the
love-based existence we were meant to live.

Fortunately, your spirit team members are highly capable of dealing with and easing all types of pain. In this chapter I will address
how angels and guides help those who need physical healing and

those who seek relief from stress, anxiety, fear, and depression. Soon you will understand how we all have the tools we need to free ourselves from the mind's pain, begin to heal, and find peace—no matter what's happening around us.

If you are hurting, as so many of us around the world are, please read this chapter with care. Venture on the healing path that angels and guides have paved for you, and I promise that you will be propelled farther than you may have thought possible. The journey may not be easy, but it will be one whose yield broadens your horizons with hope. So now, take the hand of your guardian angel and begin your first big step together toward healing you.

FINDING PEACE DESPITE A LOVED ONE'S PAIN

Now let's turn our attention to one of the most insidious and demanding sources of pain: the suffering of someone you love. Watching a loved one suffer, especially a parent, spouse, or child, can turn on a faucet of emotions of our gravest fears and anxieties. Sometimes we wish the pain would be ours to carry instead of the loved one's. Sometimes we are in denial. It's understandable. No one wants to see a daughter lying in a hospital bed hooked up to IVs. No one wants to see his or her spouse succumbing to addiction or dealing with a life-threatening disease.

The truth of the matter is that it is possible to find peace amid suffering, and angels can play a key role in helping you find that peace. By tapping into celestial energy you can find the fortitude you didn't know you had and form a new covenant with yourself and your loved ones. As always, it is necessary that you engage your team by asking for support, letting them know you need them for strength and peace of mind. Your spirit team will be more than happy to assist you. If you take the time, a few minutes a day either at your shrine or in your daily routine, to reach out to your angels and guides for strength and courage, they will surely bring new peace into your traumatic and deeply troubling situation.

Lucie—A Brief Case Study

Years ago, a middle-aged woman named Lucie came to me shortly after her mother was diagnosed with advanced colon cancer. She and her mother were very close, and it was almost as though she felt her own life slipping away. Gripped with fear, Lucie had no idea how to handle this deeply upsetting situation and wanted to know if I could help her mother heal.

I explained to Lucie that for healing to happen, her mother needed an alignment of her own body, mind, and soul. If all three of those are aligned with healing, *anything* can be healed. For most people, their emotions are not supportive of healing and are often what created the disease in the first place. However, in Lucie's mother's case her emotions were aligned with healing but her body was not able to heal the colon cancer. Even more importantly, her mother's soul's intention was to pass, and the cancer was a vehicle to assist in that process. Her soul was calling her home, and the colon cancer was the method to help her return to the other side of the veil. The painful cancer served as a means for Lucie's mother to release her journey in her earthly body in this dimension.

I counseled Lucie to ask her celestial team to help her find peace and acceptance with the eminent passing of her mother. They would be able to guide Lucie in the best way to support her mother and find personal acceptance.

To gain more insight into how Lucie dealt with her mother's cancer, I'll let her tell her story:

My mother and I had always been as close as two people can be. Growing up, my dad wasn't around, so Mom wore all kinds of hats: parent, best friend, confidant. So you can imagine the impact the words *stage-four colon cancer* had on me. It was as if all my fears and insecurities were suddenly brought to the surface. I was a little kid again, just wanting to be held by my mother, but this time around, of course, I had to be the one doing the holding.

Luckily I was already in contact with my celestial team, and I appealed to them for assistance. I had a huge ball of fear sitting in the pit of my stomach and I needed it to go away so I could be strong for my mother when she needed me—and find lasting peace when she finally passed on.

My angelic team came to my aid in the most amazing ways. Days when I visited my mom at the hospital she would often be chipper and pain-free, even though the nurses told me the day before she had been struggling. Sometimes when I was sitting at her bedside, so tired that my vision was blurring, I would receive a shot of energy and was able to talk to Mom for a few more hours, sharing memories and stories that bonded us.

But the biggest help from my team was in removing my fear of the future. Knowing that I had celestial backup allowed me to face each new and challenging situation without feeling overwhelmed and alone. That was what helped me find peace amid the destroyer of dreams that is cancer.

After one hospital stay, Lucie's mother went into remission, and they were able to spend a lot of quality time together, connecting in ways they never had before the diagnosis. But her mother's cancer returned, as cancer has a way of doing. This time, both mother and daughter accepted that this would be the end of their physical journey together—that her mother's time to cross over into a different plane of existence had come. Aided by her celestial team, Lucie accepted this without fear in her heart. Their last days together were happy ones. This would have never been possible without her angels' loving support.

When her mother did finally die, since not even angels can prevent death, Lucie, of course, missed her mother, but felt no anger or regret. By eliminating fear from her life and replacing it with love she was able to accept the reality of finite existence on this earthly plane. Instead of the paralyzing grief so many experience, she was able to embrace gratitude, thanks to the awesome healing power of angels.

ASKING TO BE HEALED

It's crucial to remember that angels and spirit guides aren't interventionists: they need you to ask them for help. They won't infringe on your free will and jump in to intervene, even if your choices are leading you down a path of suffering. It's similar to a very wise, loving parent who watches their child learn to tie their shoelaces by themselves. The parent knows that even if the child gets the laces tangled up in knots, there's nothing wrong with that. It's all part of the learning process. But when their child asks for help, then the parent steps in and assists the child in a supportive way.

Our spirit team knows that we learn through experiences, especially the painful ones. We grow through adversities and challenges. Some of our most difficult situations are often our greatest teachers. That's why our angels and guides do not judge us or interfere. They patiently wait for us to ask for their help.

Aldi—A Brief Case Study

As you can imagine, when you ask for the assistance of your angels, astounding things happen. Take the story of a young man named Aldi. Aldi was addicted to food and not surprisingly was very overweight. He had been an emotional eater for many years and used food as a source of comfort, and as a result felt great shame and profound self-hatred.

When Aldi came to me for assistance I was able to help him see things in a different way. I explained that he was an old soul who was here on Earth school to master greater levels of self-love. To help him accomplish this goal his soul had deliberately chosen to be born into a family of younger souls where he would be conditioned to believe that he was unlovable and would never measure up.

He came from a family of overeaters, and like his family, Aldi used food to suppress his pain. It was Aldi's soul's intention for him to experience obesity resulting from his addiction to food. I told Aldi it was time now to overcome his addiction and love his body rather than abuse it by overconsuming comfort food. Now his soul wanted him to heal his self-hatred so he could love himself exactly the way he was, whether he was overweight or fit.

With this new awareness Aldi saw his struggles as necessary to help him learn to love himself—even the parts of himself that he detested. He realized that to truly love himself he first needed to lovingly nurture his body. As Aldi explained,

Ever since I was a boy, food was a comfort to me. I wasn't what you might call "sociable" at school. At recess and lunch I was always alone; I didn't have the confidence to join in with my classmates. I would sit by myself and watch the world swirl around me, observing but not participating. I didn't participate in sports or other school activities. My life was that of a moviegoer with a jumbo popcorn and big-gulp soda—food was my companion while I watched life go by.

Of course, the pounds piled on. I weighed 250 pounds before I was out of high school, which only made my social anxiety worse. I would walk through the lunchroom, convinced every eye was trained on my jiggling rolls of fat. I just knew that every girl found me repulsive. I wouldn't even talk to a girl, not on your life. Twinkies and pizza slices were my friends instead.

Over the years this anxiety compounded, and I continued to use food as my crutch. I'd always been smart and gotten good grades. I was a typical weirdo with no social life. But right out of college I was hired by a big engineering company. I got a great job and plenty of money, but I was still an unlovable lump.

The anxiety of dealing with seemingly well-adjusted coworkers, confident in their slim, toned bodies, made me retreat further into myself. I had no time for gym rats, and they had no time for me. My food escape became a full-blown addiction. At one point I was consuming five thousand calories a day. Every moment of stress or challenge was immediately converted into anxiety. Like any addict, I deadened those feelings with my drug of choice: a sugary soft drink or a candy bar. Clearly, something needed to change.

But what? And how?

After talking with Robbie, I understood why I had gone down the path of addiction and self-loathing, and now it was time to turn it around. I asked my angels to help me. I told them, *I am now willing to release my cravings for the food I know I do not need. I ask in return for true fulfillment, peace, and health. Please dissolve my unhealthful attachments and adjust my cravings so I can embrace life-affirming behavior and healthy food and drink. Please help me deeply love myself.*

I'm happy to report that Aldi shed over one hundred pounds and is now, at the age of thirty-five, dating for the first time. Imagine never getting to experience something so pure and beautiful as your first kiss because you were trapped inside your own body, a prison of your own making, as Aldi was.

If we allow ourselves to be healed by angels, an entirely new world can open up, free of all the constraints that illness and addiction impose on our lives. Letting our pain be relieved by those on the celestial plane is critically important for self-discovery, self-growth, and self-love. When we permit ourselves to be healed in a deep way, we are performing a radical act of self-care and self-awareness.

By letting the angels help you heal, you acknowledge that you believe yourself worthy of being healed, which of course you are. Admitting that to yourself—truly proclaiming your own worth—is immensely challenging for many people. Trust me, once you do, and once you feel the angels' energy, you will be eternally grateful to your celestial team. You will also discover that, as the saying goes, the sky's the limit.

RELIEF IN AN INSANE WORLD

Nobody needs to convince you that this world is crazy: all you have to do is turn on the TV or click an app on your phone, and a steady stream of violence, corruption, and head-scratching events will be beamed directly into your brain. This pervasive insanity manifests a plethora of phobias, diseases, and social ills that can permeate our personal lives.

When the fate of the world dangerously careens around in our psyches, it seems nearly impossible to carve out a piece of sanity for ourselves. Take, for example, Janie's story. Janie endured years of migraines, unaware that they were caused by her way of coping with an out-of-control world. She's a perfectionist, overcommitting herself to activities and always putting other people's needs ahead of her own.

Janie—A Brief Case Study
As Janie reported to me:

I was always the best student in class and the caretaker in my home, even though I had two parents and an older sister. When I looked in the mirror I didn't see myself, but rather the person I thought I should become. Nothing was ever good enough. I was always striving to make others happy, never paying attention to my own desires or wants.

By the time I got to college the constant need to be perfect and make everyone around me happy caused my head to feel like it was literally exploding. Migraines plagued me throughout college and graduate school, rendering me totally useless for hours or days on end. Migraines cause physically and mentally debilitating pain that I wouldn't wish on anybody and can often last for days.

Desperately seeking relief, Janie contacted me for a consultation. Once I heard her story, I explained that she needed to overcome a mindset that was sabotaging her health and peace of mind. I was sure that this was at the emotional root of her migraines. Janie needed to realize that her low self-esteem and lack of love for herself caused her to neglect her own needs. She would also have to recognize and release her drive for perfection and set more realistic goals. If she was going to find peace and achieve well-being, she would have to accept the chaos of the world as an essential part of the human experience. Importantly, it was time to listen and respond to her own emotional and physical needs. Janie had to find a better balance by setting boundaries out of self-love and self-protection.

I further elaborated that when we feel negative emotions such as fear and anxiety, those emotions generate cells that are imperfect and low-functioning. They emit a lower vibration and a chemical response that produces an unhealthy environment in the body, which becomes the perfect breeding-ground for disease. Continually thinking negative thoughts can be toxic to the body and lead to disease over time.

For example, fibromyalgia is often created by consistently engaging in fearful thoughts that, unreleased, become trapped throughout the entire body. Fibromyalgia, a very painful condition of unknown origin, indicates systemic toxicity. Shame, guilt, and self-hatred are the hardest emotions for the body to process and can cause the most damage.

On the flip side, I explained to Janie how love-based thoughts and emotions create an entirely different chemical response throughout the body, producing vital, high-functioning cells that radiate at a higher vibration and frequency. The result is like a flowing, thriving river teeming with vibrant energy. I told Janie the best emotions to help her heal are gratitude and forgiveness for all, especially for herself.

Janie needed to gain awareness of what types of emotions she was "feeding" her body on a regular basis that were undermining her health and well-being. Her body was a messenger alerting her to when she was off-track. Through her migraines her body was telling her that it could no longer handle the anxiety. Thankfully, her spirit team could help her gain awareness of the mindset that was undercutting her health and replace it with a different perspective that would help relieve her anxiety.

I explained that although she could ask her angels and guides to heal her migraines immediately, they would not do so until she understood the message behind the migraines and took measures to rectify the situation. They would never interfere with the soul's intentions. To achieve release from Janie's painful migraines, her angels and spirit guides could provide motivation and guidance on creating a more balanced lifestyle. They could also help her love herself more deeply and find peace living in a chaotic world. Only *then* would her spirit team be able to help her heal, because she would no longer need the migraines to show her that she needed to change her distorted beliefs, which were the root of her problem.

Here's what Janie reported after our consultation:

It wasn't until I started communicating with angels that I was able to rid myself of these migraines. To fully heal I had to realize that to take care of myself I had to stop trying to take care of everyone else. I had to put myself first sometimes, and especially to allow myself to fail, to be an imperfect being. Knowing that I had a team of angels that loved me unconditionally was the main factor that helped me in this life-changing realization and behavioral transition. They didn't care if I was imperfect, so why should I?

I still get an occasional migraine, but I'm light years better than I was a few years ago. Being in contact with my celestial team made me realize that the only sanity you have in this mixed-up world is the sanity you carve out for yourself. I would have never realized that if it weren't for my angels.

HEALING GENERATIONS
OF DISEASE

The modern world demands so much from us. Gone are the days when well-defined roles, however restrictive, govern our existence. Now we are expected to be perfect parents, successful professionals, and talented hobbyists. The list goes on and on. Furthermore, in a society obsessed with materialism and exterior markers of success, we put enormous pressure on ourselves to meet certain societal norms. Far too often our lives are measured in terms of dollars earned, cars purchased, expensive jewelry, or status at a company. The values of our exterior world eclipse the importance of the interior world, making us unable to listen to our souls.

Living this rat race can have disastrous effects on our connection to our spiritual selves. As a result, mental-health issues like depression and anxiety, and stress-induced conditions such as heart disease and cancer are at an all-time high. Our work weeks are getting longer, and even when we are at home we are tied to our new overlords: the smartphone, which constantly beeps out some new crisis, personal or impersonal. The problem has gotten so all-encompassing that the French government felt compelled to pass a law mandating that companies can no longer force employees to check their work email past 7 p.m. Imagine if they passed that law in New York, "the city that never sleeps." The entire city might come to a halt!

Alan—A Brief Case Study

Speaking of New York, I want you to hear Alan's story. Alan presented a perfect example of someone who *seems* fine on the outside but is truly struggling inside. As he relates,

> I'm from New York. I think fast, talk fast, even eat fast. How could I get depressed? I didn't have time for depression.
>
> Let me slow down and back up for a second. I was forty-five years old, more than halfway through a promising career managing a firm that refurbished the interiors of Manhattan hotels. Hardly thrilling stuff, but it paid big bucks. I had the right house, the right car, and a gorgeous wife. My kids were in private schools, and men and women seemed to pay respect to me when I walked through the office.
>
> Even though I was living the life I had been told would make me happy, I never felt complete. Something was always missing. One day while I was shaving, I suddenly saw myself in the mirror and didn't like what I saw. I then felt an incredible weight on my shoulders. It was as if someone had dumped a load of concrete on my back. Maybe it had been there all along and I had been ignoring it, but one thing was for sure: there was no ignoring it anymore.
>
> I didn't know it at the time, but that weight is called *depression*. I thought maybe it was caused by the years and years of

pressure that the rat race had heaped on me. I didn't know how to handle it and went into a blue funk. I started drinking hard and, I'm ashamed to admit, even cheated on my wife, which I'd never done before.

One day, Alan called me searching for a way to lift himself out of his long-term depression. I explained that his depression was something his soul deliberately wanted him to experience. His soul had chosen to heal the depression that had run in his family for several generations. After we talked awhile he reluctantly agreed that his father had suffered from depression and his grandfather had committed suicide. Clearly, there was a family history of depression.

To help him better understand, I detailed how scientists had conducted studies on mice and discovered that we carry our ancestors' experiences in our cellular memory and DNA. The scientists found that mice love cherries and almonds, so that became the basis for clinical experiments. While the lab mice smelled the scent of either cherries or almonds, researchers would administer electric shocks to them. Even when the mice stopped being electrically shocked, they understandably became extremely anxious whenever they smelled cherries or almonds. Most tellingly, the researchers discovered that all the descendants of the electrically shocked experimental mice also had intense anxiety whenever they smelled cherries or almonds, even though they had never actually experienced being electrically shocked themselves.

Alan did not realize that he had deliberately chosen to incarnate into a particular genetic lineage of depression in order to be the one to finally heal it. His depression was caused by cellular memory generated on his paternal side. By healing his own depression he would be able to free his ancestors and descendants. Although his mind tried to convince him otherwise, he was in fact quite capable of completely healing his depression. He had evolved enough as a soul, plus he had all the help he needed from the other side available to him at any given time. Of course he needed to ask for the help of his spirit team before they could intervene.

I'll let Alan relay the rest of his story in his own words:

It wasn't until I relinquished control to a higher power and actually asked for help that I was able to lift that black cloud of depression off my shoulders. Lord knows I couldn't lift it by myself. That sort of thinking had gotten me into this mess in the first place, thinking I could take on the world alone.

Admitting to being depressed wasn't an easy thing for me. I'm a tough guy, y'know? But having angels and guides on my side made me able to accept the reality of my situation and accept that I needed help. That was easier than trying to bear the weight by myself. It was too heavy a load for one man to carry, but just enough for me to handle with the help of my spirit team.

So I asked my angels and guides to help me alleviate my depression and find lasting happiness. It took a few months, but I noticed that the heaviness was gradually lifting and I was experiencing moments of genuine happiness more often. I started to find joy in the simplest things, like a sunset or my wife's laughter. I knew my angels and spirit guides were behind my shift to finally release my depression for good.

The pressures of life can snowball until they turn into an avalanche of mental anguish, but your spirit team has the power to help. Don't expect to have all your problems solved immediately. Stepping off the hamster wheel of life takes time, but I promise you will see steady progress once you've engaged your angels' assistance. With their help you'll notice that over days, weeks, months, and even years you are changing. And that's a very good thing.

Finally, I want to make one point abundantly clear: angels and guides can help you heal *any* emotional malady if it's your soul's intention, and in my experience it usually is. Whether you are struggling with a small psychological hang-up or the ravages of cancer, there is simply no limit to the range and extent of their assistance. Remember, angels' primary mission is to do whatever it takes to bring this planet to a peaceful, love-based existence. They cannot do that if so many of us are suffering.

Reach out to your team for help with any pain emanating from your body or mind. You have nothing to lose and everything to gain. Angels are unlimited beings, and your pain has a limit. It will bend to the awesome power that is right within your grasp. Reach out for help from your angels and guides, who are always nearby. Their unwavering and powerful support is yours for the asking.

∞

6

Help in Challenging Situations

Being deeply loved by someone gives you strength, while loving someone deeply gives you courage.

LAO TZU

෬

*L*ife continuously challenges us with situations that seem impossible to handle, situations that assail our hearts and minds. As a result we can be stretched to the breaking point by the commonplace or the catastrophic. For example, a quarrel with a loved one can cause as much or more distress than a car accident. While there is no limit to the joy our hearts can bring us, our capacity for delight comes with an equal capacity for suffering. Our lives, our loves, our emotions often seem too much to bear, as though the weight of the universe has been heaped on our shoulders.

It doesn't have to be this way. You do not have to struggle alone in the world. In fact, you are probably creating more pain and struggle than your soul ever intended. I'm going to show you how angels are devoted to mending the distressed and the broken-hearted, and how you can channel their devotion into actionable change.

Even the most distressed readers, given a clear understanding of how their angels can aid in mending damaged relationships, can allow their hearts to become open to love once again. You will also discover how angelic assistance can bring you peace and acceptance even in the most challenging circumstances, both personally and professionally.

The main thing to remember is that angels are constantly moving us toward the love-based fifth dimension (see appendix, The Dimensions Explained). The angels' mission is to help humanity realize its essential divinity.

As you move through the challenges that life can, and will, throw at you, remember to make use of the help available from your spirit team. They love you with a love so fierce and intense that it's like staring at the sun.

FINDING LOVE AFTER HEARTBREAK

We've all been there: that sinking, horrible feeling when you first realize that a relationship is over. Whether or not you are the instigator of the breakup, the result is the same—your life changes irrevocably. The very foundation on which you built your life shifts, and you may be left feeling unwanted, unloved, and lost.

When you're on the receiving end of a breakup, the heartbreak can be excruciating. Self-esteem plummets, weight dramatically fluctuates, stress and lost sleep are constant. We've all seen movies where the spurned lover weeps into a pillow, an empty Haagen-Dazs ice cream container on the coffee table and empty liquor bottles littering the kitchen counter. When your world seems compressed into a solid vale of sadness and pain, your angels and spirit guides can be called on to take you to a beautiful place once again filled with love.

Elayna—A Brief Case Study (Part 2)

Let's return to Elayna, whom we met in chapter 4. Her concern was paying for her daughter's college tuition. I first met Elayna a few years after her husband had left her. She came to me seeking emotional support, which she needed urgently. At our initial counseling session in my office she poured her heart out. Here's what she told me:

> My husband's leaving was a tremendous shock, even though we'd been having issues for years. I thought that's what a marriage was, that we would continue like that forever, or at least until our daughter was an adult. But he pulled the trigger and disappeared from my life in what felt like an instant, our twelve-year marriage put out on the curb like a bag of trash.
>
> I was deeply hurt. The rejection was beyond painful. I thought, *What man would want me now?* I was past forty, past my prime, broke and alone. I was sure I would be single forever. I felt robbed of the possibility of romantic love. The day he left I felt as though I had awakened as one person and gone to bed as another woman—one who had wasted her life and would now spend the rest of her days as a single mom.

Immediately I spotted two flaws in Elayna's thinking. First, she considered her marriage to be a waste. Second, she had convinced herself that her romantic life had ended forever. Both assumptions were far from being the reality of her situation.

I told Elayna that the years she had spent with her ex-husband were actually part of her soul's desire and that there was an intentional purpose to that experience. I explained that her soul had deliberately chosen to be in a marriage that was not meant to be permanent in order for her to learn what she really deserved from a partner. Rather than wasted, that time was *instructional.* Coming to this realization was crucial for Elayna. It allowed her to stop berating herself over her past decisions and see them as part of a larger plan for her life, one rooted in her essential divinity.

Once she accepted this truth it was much easier for Elayna to imagine a future where she might love and be loved again. If the purpose of her marriage was to learn what she really needed from a partner, then surely she would find that partner. This is when she needed to turn to her celestial advisory team. I explained to Elayna that her angelic guides wanted nothing more than to see her living a life filled with love. Since romantic love was the type of love her soul required to fulfill its purpose, her angels were going to help her find it.

I instructed Elayna to be on the lookout for any messages or guidance her angels might be trying to give her. Her grief made her hesitate, but she finally agreed to try. Two months later I received a phone call from a very different-sounding Elayna, who ecstatically told me she was seeing someone new. She was happier than she had ever been. How had this happened?

As it turns out, Elayna's angels had stepped in when she needed them most. For days the word *illuminate* had been popping into her head at all hours of the day. While in the shower, washing the dishes, or getting dressed in the morning, she kept seeing in her mind's eye the word *illuminate . . . illuminate . . .*

Then one night the power went out in her apartment building. As she was searching for a candle, she heard a knock at her door. She opened it to find a man she had noticed who also lived in her building, holding a flashlight. He clicked it on, illuminating his kind face. "Thought you could use some help," he told her. She invited him in to thank him for his kindness, and soon they began seeing each other.

As of this writing, they have been happily married for some time. Elayna's story goes to show that when angels speak to you it pays to listen!

FINDING CELESTIAL HELP WITH YOUR MARRIAGE

Thankfully, not all romantic partnerships are destined to end. Often our celestial team leads us to our soul's intended long-term or short-term partner. I believe that you always know, deep down, if you are with the right person. Your angels can help you strengthen your relationship and smooth out the bumps along the way if that is your soul's desire. Marriages are complicated unions that require patience, tenderness, fortitude, and courage. There is no guidebook for a healthy marriage, only guideposts such as kindness, understanding, and empathy.

Dave—A Brief Case Study

I want to let a client named Dave tell you his story of how appealing to his spirit team saved his marriage:

Whew, where to begin? I suppose I should just get the bombshell out of the way right off the bat. I learned that my wife was having an affair, and with my coworker! A nightmare, right? For a while I felt like the ground had shifted beneath my feet and I was about to be swallowed up into some dark place.

When you find out that your wife has been unfaithful, a lot of things run through your mind. You feel rudderless, betrayed, less of a man. You feel extreme anger. Frankly, you want to punch the other guy in the face, or worse. In your alone, sad moments you want to disappear somewhere, like a wounded animal.

These reactions are all natural, but you also need to be rational about the situation. Ask yourself and her some basic questions, like is she in love with the other guy? How long have they been seeing each other? These are hard questions to ask and even harder answers to hear. But only with honest answers will you have any shot at forgiveness. And, trust me, forgiveness is the only way forward.

However, I was deeply hurt and angry and I sure wasn't in a forgiving mood when I called Robbie Holz. I wanted to leave my wife. Thankfully, Robbie had more foresight than I did.

"Your guides are telling me," said Robbie, when we spoke over the phone, "that your soul intends for you to forgive your wife and stay in this marriage."

"What?" I replied, aghast. "She cheated on me! And with someone I work with, some lowlife I used to consider a friend!"

Robbie explained that because it was both of our souls' intention to stay together in marriage, the angels would be allowed to help us repair the relationship. The angels would also be able to help us create a stronger, happier union.

I was skeptical. I didn't believe I could ever completely forgive my wife and save our marriage. But I also knew from past experience that if anyone could help us, the angels could, especially if it was the desire of both of our souls.

Slowly, over time, I was able to forgive my wife. Once I released the anger and feelings of betrayal, we went back to the way we were early-on in our marriage, when we were at our happiest. I'm thrilled to say that we are still happy and that our marriage is thriving.

Dave made the enlightened decision to forgive his wife and continue their relationship. He knew it was the right path for both him and his spouse. He just needed a little guidance and wisdom—

both things our angels have in great supply. So again, remember to call on your celestial guides in tough times. They are more than eager to help.

ACCEPTANCE OF OTHERS' CHOICES

Accepting decisions made by those close to us when we don't agree with them is one of the biggest challenges in any relationship. Watching someone consistently perform an action you believe to be in opposition to his or her happiness or well-being is extremely difficult, yet we must learn when to step back. His or her soul is on its own unique journey. Except in extreme examples, when there's a chance that they might actively harm themselves or others, trying to change them is not your job. Angels don't do that either. They respect our free will. Your family member, friend, or colleague may or may not follow the path you suggest for them. They also may or may not listen to *their* angels' guidance in pointing them in a healthier direction. Either way, it's your job to accept and love them, not control or judge them.

Marge—A Brief Case Study

I'll give you an example that many mothers may find familiar. A friend of mine named Marge was distressed by her adult daughter's dangerous and self-destructive use of drugs and alcohol. Marge visited me one day, understandably distraught. It took me some time to calm her down before we could have a coherent conversation. Finally, she told me how she just could not believe that her daughter Beth would make such risky choices.

"I need to fix her," Marge told me between sobs. "I just want to save her from herself."

I tried to comfort Marge while also giving her a way to come to the realization on her own that she could not fix her daughter. I explained to her that her daughter's soul wanted Beth to experience powerlessness through drug and alcohol addiction. Her daughter's soul was showing her what powerlessness felt like so that it could be avoided in the future. As English poet and painter William Blake wrote, "The road of excess leads to the palace of wisdom."

In the spirit of Blake, I explained to Marge that before her daughter was born she and Beth had entered into a soul contract for this lifetime. In the contract, Marge agreed to play the role of Beth's mother and to accept her daughter exactly the way she was, and not judge Beth because of her unhealthy choices. In their soul contract, Marge also agreed to unconditionally love her daughter while Beth learned to love herself. That was the path these two closely connected souls set upon before Beth entered this earthly plane.

I suggested to Marge that she ask her angelic team to guide her as to the best way to deal with Beth, and how to find peace of mind despite her daughter's behavior.

A few months later I saw Marge again. This time she was entirely different from the frustrated, struggling woman who had come to my home. When I commented on the change, she told me she had reached out to her team and they had provided her with what she called "an epiphany." Marge said that she came to understand that while there are far healthier and better choices, there are no mistakes. *Everything* is a learning experience. In fact, the most painful experiences are usually our best teachers.

Marge now understood that while it looked like her daughter was not learning the lessons from her addictions, she was in fact "getting it" on a deep, subconscious level and would carry that knowledge forward into future lifetimes.

Despite Beth's current continued alcohol and drug abuse, Marge and her daughter are closer than ever. Marge accepts Beth as she is and no longer engages in controlling behavior, which although well-meant, only alienated Beth in the past. Although Marge may not like her daughter's addictive lifestyle, she has made peace with Beth's choices.

DEALING WITH A TROUBLED WORLD

Any thinking person would be concerned about the state of the world today. There are so many major issues—war, terrorism, climate change, pollution, poverty, racism, animal abuse, and a range of human-rights abuses. The list of disturbing and seemingly inexplicable evil acts committed by members of the human race is endless. Think about it for too long and you're bound to feel sad, frustrated, and helpless.

That's the predicament a young man named Timothy found himself in shortly after finishing college. Timothy is exceptionally bright and doesn't like his ideas being misrepresented, so I'll let him explain:

Timothy—A Brief Case Study

You know how teenagers are fond of saying, "Screw the world"? Well, I meant it. I hated the killing of animals for fun or for their fur or tusks. I hated our senselessly polluting the natural world. My views didn't fit in with my family: my dad is a staunch conservative, avid hunter, and gun enthusiast. I also hated my awful job. So soul-crushing!

I was getting so bitter and depressed about living on this troubled planet, I knew I needed help. So, I called Robbie Holz to seek her guidance.

Robbie reminded me that Earth is a learning lab where souls bravely incarnate for tremendous growth opportunities. We're here to discover our divine nature. We're not here to save Gaia; Gaia is here to save us. Gaia, from the ancient Greek, is the ancestral mother of life. This world is all an illusion staged for the benefit of developing our consciousness.

Robbie explained how the human race has entered into a collective agreement to play different roles and go through specific experiences for the benefit of raising individual and collective consciousness. She assured me everyone has agreed to these experiences, including wildlife. Whether victim of an oil spill, mass shooting, or rape, we each have subconsciously agreed to be a participant. Sometimes we may be clearing karma. Usually we are experiencing what is needed to help us evolve into higher consciousness.

She then described the hundredth-monkey theory, which means that once a critical number of members of one group exhibit a new behavior or accept a new idea, the new behavior or idea spreads from one group to other related groups. This phenomenon was discovered by scientists studying snow monkeys who inhabited a Japanese island. They observed that one monkey taught another monkey to wash sand off sweet potatoes in the ocean. The second monkey then taught another, who taught another, and so on. And thus the idea spread. Soon all the monkeys on the island were washing sand off their sweet potatoes in the ocean. When the hundredth monkey learned the process, it spread to monkeys across the globe, who all began spontaneously washing their food as well. It was a sudden leap of worldwide consciousness, achieved when a critical mass was reached. When a tipping-point is reached, as in the hundredth monkey, the new idea or innovation becomes part of the collective consciousness of all. Of course, this theory applies to humankind as well.

In that moment I understood that by raising my consciousness I would help raise the collective consciousness as well. By awakening to my true divine nature and not continuing to see myself as separate, living in duality, and by learning to transcend my conditioned responses and thoughts, I would make it easier for others to do the same. By mastering my thoughts and emotions, engaging in less fear-based negativity while living in more love-based positivity, I can achieve a higher state of consciousness.

Robbie explained how important it is to pay attention to the types of energy my thoughts and emotions create, because that not only affects me but everyone around me. Whenever I was feeling frustrated, angry, or depressed, I was energetically adding those lower-vibrational frequencies to the collective. Whenever I engage in love-based thoughts and emotions, it raises my vibration and it also raises the collective vibration.

She then suggested that if I wanted to make a positive difference in the world I should engage more often in compassion, forgiveness, and unconditional love. It would also be helpful for me to consciously hold a vision in my thoughts of the world at peace and in harmony. If I feel called to be an activist, I should act on it only because I'm responding from my heart and it feels right, not out of fear and anger. This was just what I needed to hear.

Several weeks later I received an email from Timothy. He wanted to update me on his progress. Timothy described how he asked his spirit team to help him make a positive difference in the world. Within days he noticed his emotions shifting as he became more compassionate toward people in less evolved states. He now understood that they were still in the mindset to only serve themselves and not yet in the higher consciousness of service to others.

Timothy believes it was his angels and guides who led him to a group of like-minded people helping the homeless. He enjoys the camaraderie and how uplifting the dedicated volunteers are as they quietly work behind the scenes to assist folks who need a helping hand in tough times.

Many of my readers are among those souls who have deliberately chosen to incarnate in these auspicious times as we shift from

the third dimension of being, pass briefly through the fourt
ultimately enter the fifth love-based dimension (see appendix, The
Dimensions Explained). Perhaps you feel that you don't fit into the
world around you, in what you may see as an extremely primitive
planet. Perhaps you don't want to be here anymore. This is completely
understandable, but know this: You are here now because you have
work to do. You volunteered to plant seeds of awakening, to personally add to the tipping point that can and will raise the consciousness
of the collective. It's a harvest you may not see in your lifetime, but
perhaps those just being born now will benefit from the shift into
higher consciousness. Your soul agreed to add more forgiveness, compassion, and love energy to the collective and to the planet herself.

What an amazing time to be on Earth! No wonder you signed
up for it!

Remember who you *really* are and what you're here to do. Your
angels and guides are more than happy to assist as you move into
a higher consciousness. They will be delighted to help you release
anything that is in your best interest to release and open you up to
new and exciting possibilities. Always remember, the angelic realm
can help you live the highest vision of your soul—but first you must
ask for their help.

⌒

7

Overcoming Self-Hatred

Thinking that I'm a mistake is the real mistake.

CRAIG D. LOUNSBROUGH

∽

*A*t a low moment in life, many of us have looked in the mirror
and mouthed these three words: *I hate myself.* Whether
you've felt unqualified to apply for a job you wanted, kicked yourself for not telling someone you had a crush on them, felt helpless at
the hands of a bully, critically pinched the fat around your bulging
waistline, failed to give up drinking or some other addiction, or were
consistently late to work, occasional bouts of self-loathing are both
common and universal. They are feelings that most of us are all too
familiar with.

Many of us have no awareness of the origins of our self-hatred,
the myriad ways it shows up in our lives, and how to fortify against
it. Humanity's ignorance about the underlying causes of self-hatred is
problematic because self-hatred puts up a barrier to self-acceptance,
which is the all-important cornerstone of happiness and effectiveness
in daily life. If we ask, our spirit team will open our eyes to the truth

of the matter. As we know from the previous chapter it is a
could have massive implications for the advancement of hui
and is certainly a truth that can change *your* life.

Here is the essential truth: You are Divine Source experiencing
life as a soul incarnated in a physical body. We each exist because
Divine Source has a tremendous desire to be, to know itself, to
express, to create. Simply put, we are spiritual beings having a human
experience, not human beings having a spiritual experience.

Divine Source is everywhere and experiences itself through existence as a bird, as a mountain, or as a human. In other words, Source
seeks manifestation through you. There is no underlying difference
between you and someone else. You are a fractal of Divine Source, experiencing itself through you. It's important to understand that Divine
Source is in you because that's who you are—but Divine Source is in
others as well because that's who we all are. It's easier to recognize that
when you release the identity created by your egoic mind and release
negativity toward yourself, *especially* self-hatred and self-loathing.

To ascend to your highest level of consciousness, you need to
transform the self-hatred you may be holding onto subconsciously
into self-love. Fortunately, no matter who you are or where you are in
your life, you are beloved by your spirit team, who will help you see
yourself as the endlessly beautiful, transcendent being of light and
love that you truly are.

IMPERFECTLY PERFECT

Earlier I explained how you and every other person on this planet
are comprised of Divine Source, the most elemental component of
all things. Again, if you think of Divine Source as the ocean, you are
not merely a drop in the ocean; you are the entire ocean in a drop.
Each of us is the exact same *quality* of Divine Source, but in a smaller
quantity than Source.

Since we live on Earth it is easy to forget this essential truth. One young woman whom I'll call Sophie had forgotten this, and it nearly cost her her life. Thankfully it was her soul's intention that she carry on living. But her story is a harrowing one, and I must warn you that it contains subject matter that can trigger those who have survived sexual abuse or eating disorders. I'll let her speak to you directly:

Sophie—A Brief Case Study

After graduating from art school I moved to Brooklyn, New York, and threw all my energy into making jewelry. I was single-minded, if not obsessed, about building a business, and it did take off. I began small, selling at church bazaars and street fairs, but I was persistent, and eventually it was thrilling when boldface names, including rock stars, Hollywood A-listers, and big city "It girls" began wearing my creations to red-carpet events.

You'd think I'd be able to enjoy my success, but just the opposite happened. Due to the stress of my jewelry brand being in the public eye, the trauma of a sexual assault I had experienced when I was in art school resurfaced, and I began having overwhelming feelings of shame. I didn't feel like I deserved any of the good things in my life. I convinced myself that I was a fraud and an imposter who didn't deserve to be in the world of beautiful, successful people. Everyone I met in New York seemed so thin, so accomplished, so chic. I felt like nobody from nowhere who had tricked these glossy people into thinking that I had something to offer. I felt a tremendous amount of guilt and shame. I berated myself, *Stupid girl, at any moment someone is going to come along and discover your insignificance. You are such a fake!*

I became obsessed with my weight, too, thinking that I had to be stick-thin to fit in with the jet-set crowd. I developed an eating disorder and forced myself to throw up after meals. Eating well became a thing of the past. Instead of eating, I "did lunch" with clients at Charlie's, a bar down the street from my studio, which really just meant vodka martinis and pretending to eat olives. All too often I slipped into a state of numbness, a liquid escape from troubles that at that time I didn't even know I had.

Soon I was consuming half a bottle of vodka a day and very little else. I suffered rapid weight loss, but that's not what I saw when I looked in the mirror. I saw a distorted version of myself. I thought I looked like some kind of demon. Even my jewelry designs began to take on a sinister look: bracelets made of twisted metal that wrapped around my thin wrists like coiling vipers.

Of course, all of this was a recipe for the worst kind of disaster. After collapsing in the hallway of my studio, I ended up in the hospital. The doctors told me that I weighed only eighty-five pounds, had a severely enlarged liver, and that my heart could stop at any moment. On the verge of death, I spent over a month recovering at an eating disorder clinic in Seattle. That's where I met Robbie Holz.

I had been close to Sophie's aunt for a long time. One day she called to ask me to please meet with her niece, who was struggling with some issues. After clearing it with Sophie herself, I visited her at Opal: Food + Body Wisdom, a clinic in Seattle.

When I arrived I saw Sophie, a beautiful girl, hooked up to an IV, wasting away and having come so close to dying. I quietly slid into the chair across from her and gave her a smile. There were dark circles under her eyes. I could see that she had been through hell and sensed that she was now trying very hard to find her way back to a better life.

After we had talked for a while, I asked her point-blank, "Sophie, do you realize that you are a soul?"

With a worried brow, she replied, "I know I *have* a soul, but I don't know about *being* one. Is being my soul the same thing as being my higher self?"

"Your higher self is a smaller aspect of your soul," I explained. "Your higher self is the highest portion of you that can be contained in your human body. It's the aspect of you that sees, understands, and *knows* certain things at the highest possible level while you operate in this third dimension. Integrating your higher self's wisdom into your everyday life is a large part of your spiritual growth and evolution."

"Your soul is different than your higher self," I continued. "Your soul plays a major role in deciding and designing what you experience in each lifetime. Your soul wants to go through particular events as part of its evolution, so it puts a plan in place and the process for these experiences to happen to you. In other words, your life's journey will reflect what your soul wants to master. We are always here to learn. That's why the same growth opportunities show up on your path over and over again—to help you get better at things like forgiveness, acceptance, and self-love. The soul is an eternal divine essence that inhabits the body and acts through it. Like the strings on a marionette, the soul is the animating force. When the strings are cut, the marionette collapses."

"Okay," Sophie said, listening thoughtfully.

"Think of the soul as you might think of electricity for a light bulb or software for a computer," I continued. "The soul is the animating principle."

"Okay, I get it. I have a soul," Sophie said softly.

"Not exactly. You don't *have* a soul. You *are* a soul. That is a big distinction. You *have* a body."

"Oh. Yes, I see the difference," Sophie said.

"Your soul is passionate about evolution. That's why your soul chooses to reincarnate over many, many, many lifetimes," I said.

"My soul doesn't die?" Sophie asked.

"Right. Your soul is eternal. All bodies eventually die, bᵤ carry on. Sophie, your life reflects the continuity of your sou., ᵤₒᵢₙg one body after another for the purpose of soul growth, expanding into higher consciousness and gaining increasing awareness of your essential divine nature. When a human dies, the soul leaves the physical body but continues on as an etheric spirit, a being of love and light in a different dimension than the earthly realm."

"I'm not sure I understand what my soul wants me to learn," Sophie said.

"Your soul wants you to learn how to love yourself more. This lifetime for you is about mastering deeper levels of self-love."

Sophie's hand quickly covered her mouth and she let out a small gasp. "I'm doing a terrible job of that." Lowering her head, I saw a single tear run down her cheek.

I waited a minute while she composed herself, then continued. "Because this journey is about developing self-love, you needed to experience circumstances that *deliberately* led you to believe you were deeply flawed and unworthy. You purposely incarnated into your specific family because they would condition you to believe you were not good enough. Your aunt told me you experienced a sexual assault in college. I know that was difficult, but that awful event was necessary to contribute to your self-image of being damaged."

I paused to let that sink in and then said, "It's time to recognize who you really are and release your distorted belief that you are inadequate and unlovable. Your soul wants you to heal this now."

"I wouldn't have the faintest idea how to love myself," Sophie said, looking around the room. "My Lord, look around—I'm in rehab, for goodness sakes! Obviously I'm pretty clueless about taking care of myself."

"For starters, loving yourself is the absence of negative thoughts about yourself. That means no self-judgment, harsh inner criticism, and comparisons to others," I replied.

"That's all I've done since I was a kid," Sophie mused.

"Although it's very common in our culture, it's actually childish and immature. That negativity really needs to stop," I said firmly.

"I never thought of my inner critic as childish and immature," Sophie said.

"You're designed *exactly* the way you need to be according to your soul's intentions for what you're here to learn in this lifetime. If you needed to be different, you'd be different."

Sophie's mouth dropped open.

"Your soul has so many things it wants to experience through you, Sophie. And it has a tremendous role in deciding what you will experience in each lifetime. Your soul chooses a body to perfectly fit those learning experiences. Like everyone else, you're designed to have both shadow and light in your life to create contrast. Just as in an oil painting, contrast makes it easier to see things more clearly. Sophie, you need the shadow aspects of yourself so you can see and understand things better.

"Souls *love* incarnating on Earth to evolve for a number of reasons," I continued. "First, it's a free-will planet, which means you choose how to respond to the experiences your soul establishes for you."

"It's my choice?" Sophie asked.

"Yes. You can react from your conditioned egoic mind or from your divine nature with love-based emotions like compassion, patience, acceptance, and forgiveness. It's more than just free will that draws souls here, Sophie. It's the extreme diversity of younger souls, older souls, and everything in between—the dark and the light—that provides endless opportunities for growth."

"What's a younger soul like?" she queried.

"Younger souls tend to be greedy, materialistic, and self-serving. Older souls are often more loving and compassionate, with a greater desire to help others. We're all at different stages of soul development. The older soul may be more enlightened and have more growth under its belt, but that doesn't mean it is better than the younger, less-evolved soul. Every one of us will reach higher consciousness and enlightenment eventually. It's not uncommon for an older soul to incarnate into a family of younger souls, as you have. There is a master plan about how souls come together in a family or in other relationships. We have a lot to teach one another."

"I see. We're souls and we learn from each other," Sophie remarked.

"Exactly! We are all souls in Earth school together. And we all have lessons to master in this lifetime. Think of this, Sophie, as obtaining your Ph.D. in self-love. Your soul very carefully set you up with a specific body and with a family with a limiting belief system that conditioned you to believe you weren't worthy of love. Your soul intended for you to buy into it all, and you did. You needed to experience all of it. There are no mistakes. Some of the most painful experiences are our best teachers and motivate us to change. We learn from *everything* and carry that knowledge forward eternally as a soul. But now, Sophie, it's time to realize who you really are: a fractal of Divine Source, an extraordinary divine luminous being, incredibly brave for incarnating on this tough, primitive planet."

"I feel so broken," Sophie began to cry.

"You don't need to be fixed. You're perfect exactly as you are. Embrace what you think of as your flaws and imperfections. They are all necessary. It's your mind that is misleading you, making you believe you're defective. Your mind has taken over and has been sabotaging you. It's time to take back control!"

"How in the world do I control my mind?" Sophie dabbed her eyes. "You don't know how strong my mind is. Look where it got me."

"Your mind needs to be redirected so that it's helping you rather than creating havoc. It's a matter of training your mind to respond in a new way. Let me use my dog Checkers as an example of how to

passed years ago. Checkers was such a sweetheart. He
[...]-sized springer spaniel, smart as a whip and extremely
[...] us. Checkers always wanted to be involved in whatever
I was doing. To his canine mind he was being tremendously helpful,
even when he wasn't."

"I had a dog like that. Buster was always underfoot," Sophie
chimed in, relating to my story.

"During a bad storm, a massive tree crashed through our bedroom ceiling. Naturally, we had to have the roof and ceiling repaired.
In the midst of the repairs, Checkers was in the middle of the bedroom along with the carpenters, Sheetrock guys, and painters. Even
though he was a nuisance, in everyone's way, Checkers was convinced
he was helping. If I were to lock Checkers out of the bedroom or the
house, he would scratch at the door, bark, and make things worse.

"Checkers needed to be involved in a way that was helpful. So
I put him by the front door which was near the bedroom and had
him be a guard dog, alerting us when the workers showed up. He
was happy because he was doing something he was good at and I was
happy because he was actually assisting. Checkers needed to be *redirected*. In our family, when you think you're helping but you're really
not, like clearing someone's dishes off the dining room table before
they are finished eating, we call that 'Checkers-helping.' Sophie,
your mind has been 'Checkers-helping' and needs to be redirected
so it's being helpful instead of landing you in more life-threatening
circumstances."

I saw Sophie's eyes widen with recognition and relief.

"My mind needs to be involved but I have to redirect it," Sophie
repeated.

"Exactly. This journey is about learning how to control your
mind rather than your mind controlling *you*. Certain thoughts have
become habitual, but any habit can be changed."

"How do I do that?" Sophie asked.

"First, become aware when your mind is presenting you with negative, fear-based thoughts. That's pure Checkers-helping. Pay attention to what triggered it. We're most vulnerable to the mind's negative antics when we're tired. That's why I do not allow my mind to have center stage when I'm tired, especially at night. That's just asking for trouble!"

"Gain awareness," said Sophie softly.

"Right. You're too often on autopilot. Be more mindful and more conscious. Our minds are incredibly powerful, so it's important to become aware of unhealthy thoughts and steer them into healthier ones that support you. Redirect your mind away from fear and negativity into love-based emotions such as gratitude, acceptance, and forgiveness. Ask if what your mind is telling you is really true. Just because you think something doesn't mean it's true. It's just a thought. Thoughts and feelings constantly come and go. Observe your mind—but don't identify with it. It's not who you are."

"My mind is always reliving the past," said Sophie.

"That's often abusive. Don't allow your mind to take you down dark alleys of the past or even into the future. Stay in the present moment—that's where your power is, because that's where you create, and the present moment is all there really is. Live in the present. The rest will take care of itself."

Sophie emitted a long, deep sigh. "My mind is strong, but I'm going to do my best to control it, now that I know my life depends on it."

"You've identified with your mind's falsehoods and lies for a long time. At times it's taken you over and you've become a slave to it. Learning to control your mind is like learning a new skill. It's a little awkward in the beginning, but it gets better with practice. Be patient and gentle with yourself while you learn how to redirect your Checkers-helping mind into more love-based thoughts. One thought at a time, you've got to retrain your mind on how to love yourself."

"I want to start liking myself, even the shadow parts," Sophie said thoughtfully. "But it's going to be really hard."

"Don't let your mind tell you it's going to be really hard. Don't buy into that. You're equipped to handle whatever your soul signed you up for. Plus, you always have the angelic help you need. It was never intended for you to do this alone."

As Sophie listened, I described how everyone on the planet has at least one guardian angel by his or her side, waiting to be asked to assist. I explained how she has tremendous help available to her from the other side of the veil in many forms but guardian angels are the easiest to communicate to and build a relationship with. I told Sophie how her guardian angel could help her learn to love herself and fulfill all the requirements for a Ph.D. in self-love. I explained in detail how to hand anything and everything over to her guardian angel. As we were saying good-bye, I could see that something inside Sophie had shifted. Her eyes suddenly sparkled with excitement and hope.

About a year later I got a phone call from Sophie. She wanted me to know that she now understood what self-love *was* and what it *wasn't*. She knew self-love meant to eat healthy, stay sober, and let go of the past. She recognized that it was her guardian angel who was motivating her to eat better, gain weight, and exercise regularly. Sophie had no doubts that her guardian angel was also behind her desire to regularly attend AA meetings and remain sober.

She told me how she'd asked her angel to help her release hateful thoughts about herself. Although it was a work in progress, her harsh inner critic didn't get triggered as often, and far less intensely. When she slipped and began beating herself up, she caught herself and didn't stay in that dark hole for long. Since working with her guardian angel, the biggest change she noticed was that her previous judgmental attitude toward herself and others had turned into compassion and acceptance.

I told her she was well on her way to earning that advanced degree her soul intended her to obtain. She was an enlightened soul with a great deal to offer others and a wonderful future ahead of her.

UNDERSTANDING THE ROLES WE PLAY

Needless to say, our world is a vast stage, and each and every one of our souls has a unique part to play. Sometimes those roles look very different from what we might imagine or what we think they should be. Society has all sorts of rules for how we *should* live our lives. While these guidelines are often helpful, they are also far from a complete playbook on how to approach our individual existence. If you are trying to fit a round peg into a square hole, it will never fit.

Larry—A Brief Case Study

A client named Larry is a perfect example of how believing you are supposed to conform to a certain path can warp your perception of yourself, and this can lead to self-loathing. That was Larry's state of mind during our consultation. He told me how as a young married man he had been hired as a CPA at a national accounting firm. His high-profile job demanded extensive traveling, which meant he was away from his wife and two children more than he was with them. "I was the sort of dad who missed football games, birthdays, and even holidays," he told me.

Larry went on to say that his work schedule had severely damaged his marriage, that his wife resented him for being away from the family so much. "Now I sit here each day thinking that I should have done everything differently. If I could go back to the moment I accepted this job, I'd decline it in a heartbeat," he related, holding back tears. "I could have taken other CPA jobs that didn't require traveling away from my family so often, but I went for the big bucks instead. I thought I was doing the right thing for my family."

Every guilt-ridden word that Larry spoke was laden with the belief that he had screwed up and let down those he loved in some unforgivable way. Filled to the brim with doubt and grief, he blamed himself, when in reality he had actually made the choices his soul intended him to make.

I understood his situation immediately. It was clear that Larry's soul's objective in this lifetime was to master self-forgiveness. Larry's soul had intended that he would choose money over family. Realizing the consequences of his choices later in life, Larry would need to overcome painful hurtles in order to eventually forgive himself.

What would help him release his guilt was recognizing that his wife and both of their children also had soul contracts to experience a life of abandonment by him. It was what everyone needed for his or her individual growth and development.

After explaining this soul dynamic to Larry, I suggested that he engage his guardian angel to help him find compassion and self-forgiveness.

THE BLESSING OF FORGIVENESS

Early in my relationship with my celestial team they granted me a powerful epiphany of my own: I learned that the exact opposite of hatred is forgiveness. When you hate someone, including and especially yourself, that hatred consumes your being. It fills you with visions of retribution and reprisal and robs you of your essential divinity.

When you forgive someone or yourself, you release the roadblock of negativity that lives in your heart, and you initiate a huge injection of love into your immediate surroundings and into the world at large.

The domino effect created by this generous act brings the whole world closer to the tipping point that we are all eagerly awaiting. Therefore, when you forgive, you are not only doing the right thing for yourself and for others, you are performing a vital service for humanity.

Often souls take on the challenge of forgiveness both of self and of others. If it is your soul's intention to do so, in this particular lifetime be prepared to encounter situations over the span of your lifetime that require forgiveness. If you're an older soul, you may be faced with difficult circumstances that require forgiveness more than younger souls will. This is understandable. You wouldn't sign up for kindergarten classes in Earth school when you're teaching to graduate students. That was the case with an older soul I encountered named Jeremy. I'll let Jeremy tell his story:

Jeremy—A Brief Case Study

My father was cast from a mold of manhood that probably hardly exists anymore. He was a holdover from the incredibly repressed masculine image of the 1950s. At night he would come home from work smelling like gin, grunt a few words at my long-suffering mother, and after bolting down his food, take a large gin martini to the den to watch the TV news. Over time, that martini became a bottle of gin or whiskey or vodka. Over more time, a bottle of booze became two bottles.

When he was drunk, all his bottled-up emotions turned into fury, and he would lash out at those closest to him. There were many nights when I tried to get between my old man and my mother as he berated her, yelling and raising his fist while she shrank back in helpless agony. I was just a boy, so a swift push from him easily sent me flying. This was often followed by a session with his brown leather belt. That belt—how I loathed it. It's the reason I wear suspenders, even though I know they look a bit silly on me.

Though my father never said so, to me it was clear that he considered his life a bungled mess of lost opportunities, and he blamed himself for the implosion of his dreams. He made sure I knew that he considered me the heir to his throne of failure and that I felt his pain. As I sat at the kitchen table doing my homework, he would hover over me, bottle of liquor in hand. "What's the point in that?" he would sneer. "You know you'll never put it to use. You're dumb as they come, just like me."

But I wasn't just like him. I was smart. I got straight As in high school and actually graduated at the top of my class. My father missed the ceremony, passed out on the couch with a glass in his hand. After graduation I made sure to get straight out of my small town. I moved to Seattle, got a good education, worked my way through college and then law school, and made something of myself. Eventually I had a thriving practice. I vowed that I would never be like my father. And for the most part, I wasn't.

Then, unexpectedly, after he passed away, I felt some of that old anger creeping back. For some reason I began to resent my mother. Why hadn't she protected me from him all those years? Why hadn't she been stronger for herself? Why hadn't she been able to help make him into the man he wanted to become?

After speaking with Robbie, who had actually put me in touch with my spirit team years before when I needed help with another issue, I realized how important it was to forgive both my father and my mother. Robbie explained that my soul needed me to gain mastery over forgiveness. That was one of my soul's important lessons. She also told me that because I am an older, more developed soul, my "forgiveness lessons" would be more difficult than most. My soul chose my path, growing up with an abusive father and a passive mother. Both parents would provide plenty of opportunities for me to either forgive them or hold on to resentment. These were not just growth opportunities—these were significant opportunities!

Robbie suggested I ask my spirit team to help me forgive my parents who, I learned, were younger souls. My guides could also help me find acceptance and compassion for my parents because they hadn't learned about love. Robbie also helped me understand I was clearing karma from a past life where I had been abusive toward my spouse and children.

It didn't happen overnight, but forgiving my father and mother was one of the best decisions I've ever made. It opened me up to love and enabled me to fall in love and accept being loved. I had found this extremely difficult until I unblocked all my toxic resentment and found my true self again.

Whatever animus or hatred resides in your heart, let it go. Let love take its place. You have nothing to lose except the hatred that is holding you back in every area of your life.

SELF-LOVE INVOLVES BOUNDARIES

Now let's talk about an all-important but too often overlooked component of self-love: creating appropriate and practical boundaries. Drawing lines in the sand, so to speak, helps reduce the kind of stress, anxiety, and negativity that, left unchecked, can morph into self-loathing. We've all had a boss who demanded too much of us, a coworker who made us shoulder an unfair amount of work, or a friend who borrowed money and failed to repay it. Stoically putting up with aggression and dishonesty is not a love-based approach to existence. This kind of tolerance, which is not in our best interests, can lead to festering feelings of resentment. These in turn can initiate cycles of misunderstanding and self-hatred.

You also do not need to play the role of the rescuer. It is not your responsibility to fix or rescue another person. What you may need to do instead is to set up protective boundaries out of self-love. A friend of mine named Gabby recently discovered the truth of this when she set in place some tough rules with her mother. Here is Gabby, in her own words, explaining why it was necessary to step away, and how her guides helped her make that difficult decision.

Gabby—A Brief Case Study

Lots of women have complicated feelings toward their mothers. My relationship with my mother went beyond the normal push-pull. Simply put, I never believed that my mother loved me the way a mother should love a daughter. From a young age she constantly told me that I was ugly. She put me down in every way imaginable. She would even ask boys I was dating why in the world they would want to be with a girl like me. To say the least, it was very hurtful.

Even after I was out of the house and well into my thirties, she continued to manipulate me and try to exert control over all aspects of my life. I was losing sleep over it. Surely I should not cut off my relationship with my own mother. But then I had to ask myself why I was so set on placating a woman who quite obviously did not have my best interests at heart. What was the cost to my family and myself? I now had a daughter of my own. How was this dysfunctional relationship between her grandmother and me affecting her?

At my wit's end, I appealed to my angels for help. Lo and behold, they provided me with a clear answer. They helped me feel that yes, I did indeed need to set boundaries with my mother, and that this action on my part was necessary out of self-love.

My hands shaking, I dialed my mother's number. When she

answered, I told her she needed to make some serious ch
in the way she spoke to me and the way she treated me. I
no longer tolerate her toxic behavior. Needless to say, she hung
up on me. That click of the receiver was one of the loudest
noises I have ever heard in my life.

That was the hardest call I ever made. I have not heard from
my mother since. Perhaps she will change someday. Possibly
she won't. However, I now know that is *her* problem, not mine.
I have forgiven her in my heart, but that does not mean I need
to have her be a part of my life.

The change has been monumental for me. I'm finally free
to be the woman I wanted to be when I was younger. I believe
the little girl I once was would be proud of me and delighted
to know that our grown-up version did get to live a happy life,
free of our mother's delusional and demeaning behavior. Her
negativity had been wearing down my essence, robbing me of
my birthright—to be joyful, loving, and loved.

When Gabby set boundaries between herself and her hurtful
mother, she was able to finally live her truth. That's what this chapter and more broadly this book is all about: living your truth. If you
live your truth, guided by angels, you will not only be happier and
more fulfilled, you will have an enormously positive impact on others as well.

Today our collective human consciousness is moving us all
toward a love-based existence. You are a vital part of that consciousness. This cannot be overstated. We are all moving toward becoming
purer expressions of Divine Source.

∞

8

Finding Your
Ultimate Purpose

Be a rainbow in someone else's cloud.

MAYA ANGELOU

ॐ

Hopefully you have gained insight into how to deal with some of life's most difficult challenges. If you have made it this far, your life has already been altered in fundamental ways. *How* exactly you have been changed might still seem uncertain. Let me assure you that change *has* occurred, and will continue to take place long after you have read the final words of this book.

You may be questioning some of the worldview I present here, but you have now been made more aware of the role that angels and spirit guides play in our world. Once you accept this fundamental truth, even if your egoic mind still throws out little doubts like dangerous sparks from a fire, everything changes. A source of light, once illuminated, will always penetrate the darkness, steadily and unceasingly feeding the divine within you. That process actually began when you discovered this book.

Now that you are nearing the end of this book, an important question arises: *What next?* How do you venture out into the world using the lessons and strategies you've now learned? How will you stay connected to your new purpose-driven life while managing all the hurdles the world places on your path? How will you find your ultimate purpose? And once you've discovered it, how do you work toward it, protect it, and successfully navigate the challenges that inevitably spring up along the way? In short, how will you spend the rest of your time here on Earth?

These are tough questions. Thankfully, a few decades of working in this field have provided me with some good answers that I am happy to share and that will serve you long after you finish reading this book. The four sections of this final chapter are designed to provide you with a roadmap for the steps you will follow to keep your spirit team engaged, your consciousness evolving, and to quicken your soul's journey toward its true purpose. These steps have always been extremely helpful for me and for many of my clients. I hope they will provide you with a way to continuously strive toward wholeness, so you can persist on the path to personal and spiritual fulfillment.

KEEP EVOLVING YOUR CONSCIOUSNESS

To fulfill your soul's purpose you will need to keep raising the level of your consciousness. Actively engaging in this soul-level development will both escalate the progress of your relationship with celestial beings and enable you to express more of your true divine nature.

Becoming more open to aligned guidance from angels and guides will undoubtedly increase your consciousness. Be on the alert for their messages. As for becoming fully clairvoyant, few people are.

It's something you must be born with. However, you are naturally clairsentient, able to perceive messages from both human and non-human sources. If you work on your clairsentience, it will improve vastly over time. Your adeptness in intuitively sensing angelic guidance will grow, leading to better decision-making in all areas of your life. By making an effort to be in daily contact with the other side, the expansion of your consciousness will happen just as naturally as strengthening your muscles with regular exercise.

I've found some primary strategies for myself and others that have been useful in advancing consciousness. I believe these will prove helpful as you forge your path forward. Use them as a framework on which to build your own spiritual practice. There is no one path toward enlightenment. Think of these as open-ended suggestions on which you can superimpose your own specifics.

Open-mindedness is key. The main reason you began the journey of this book is because you are open to the idea of angels existing in the universe. You will need to employ that same open mindset as you continue your development. Do not be afraid of ideas or concepts that others shrug off. Listen to your intuition. Listen to your guides. They will show you the way.

Find others who are like-minded. For me, this was of course my beloved late husband, Gary. For you, this person could be anyone: a lover, a friend, or an online community. When interpreting the sometimes confusing messages our divine helpers send us, it is enormously helpful to run them by a trustworthy, nonjudgmental person, one who will help you recognize the truth.

Work at it as you would work at anything else. Developing your consciousness, especially with regard to communicating with angels and guides, is something that takes time and effort. It's not like riding a bike; the quality of your interaction can erode over time if you are not diligent. Think of it as a relationship like any other. You will only get as much out of it as you put into it. If you are willing to put in the effort, the rewards will be enormous, on both a personal and a planetary level.

REVEALING YOUR SOUL'S TRUE INTENTIONS

As I related at the beginning of this book, I was not always attuned to the intentions of my soul, which caused me great personal pain for a number of years. In 1985, after a difficult thirty-six-hour labor and delivery of my only child, I was given a blood transfusion that was tainted with hepatitis C. Of course, my doctors did not know this, since today's tests were not yet developed. The hep C virus lay hidden in my liver for years until it decided to declare war on my entire body, starting in 1992. Over the next five years I developed fibromyalgia, chronic fatigue syndrome, and sustained temporary brain damage. I was bedridden for many months. Traditional medicine and even cutting-edge experimental Western medicine did not work for me, and I was at a loss as to where to turn.

Because my son was so young I was determined to find a way to survive, to love and parent him. That desperate desire to live put me on an unconventional path. Because I had plumbed the depths of Western medicine, which now no longer had options for me, I sought alternative healing techniques. More importantly, I didn't know that I was on a path to healing myself emotionally and spiritually as well.

That's when I discovered the tremendous role that angels can play in healing. I realized that my soul had a plan for me. It was my soul's *intention* for me to heal. It was time to quiet my tough inner critic, to listen and respond to my body's needs, and to lovingly nurture myself back to health. No longer would I allow my fearful mind to call the shots and create an unhealthy body. I would focus on what mattered, allowing my true divine nature to emerge more fully. My life would be guided by the answer to the question *What would love do?*

My hope is that you will not have to suffer that same tug-of-war between mind and soul. However, if you are currently waging that war, please put down your weapons. You are only using them against yourself. When you face emotional and physical pain, the questions to ask yourself are: What am I resisting and why? Why is this in my path? How will these challenges help me grow?

Here's a hint: if your emotions are uncomfortable—anxiety, guilt, shame, resentment, anger, etc.—they are negatively affecting your body. Your body can't thrive, let alone heal, with this toxicity. What it boils down is this: you're either engaged in fear or in love. Love is always the answer. Make a conscious choice to shift out of negative thoughts and emotions. Engage in love-based thoughts and emotions as much as you can, especially gratitude for all the good things in your life.

It's likely some forms of emotional and physical pain have finally gotten your attention. Are you listening to your soul's voice *now*? It's attempting to steer you in a different direction than the negative path that your mind has been engaging. Listen to your soul's voice. You're going to love where it takes you!

As a younger woman, I would never have believed it was my soul's intention to receive a blood transfusion contaminated with hepatitis C. Now I know that it could not have happened any other way. I was being guided by forces I was not yet able to see. I encourage you to open yourself up to these forces and allow them to embrace you.

CONNECTING WITH THE ANGELIC REALM

My hope is that your relationship with your angels and spirit guides will continue to evolve and become the cornerstone of your life.

However, it may also be the case that your relationship with your spirit team will begin to dwindle without daily practice—a phenomenon similar to what occurs when you don't keep in touch with an old friend.

The straightforward reason: reading *Angels in Waiting* is a fully immersive process, comparable to undertaking coursework or a seminar on a specific subject. You are now most likely thinking about angels and guides, contemplating everything we've discussed and attempting to engage with them. However, for many people, once they are no longer in this "class," their focus tends to drift. They fall back into old ways of thinking and old habits. They allow the hubbub of life to crowd their thoughts until they soon realize they have fallen out of communication with their angels and guides. What was once an open channel becomes hindered.

The fact is, if you don't keep up with your angelic relationship, your celestial communication skills will become rusty. If this happens to you there is a relatively simple solution. Go back to basics and reconnect with your team in the same way that you first connected with them.

MOVING INTO THE LOVE-BASED
FIFTH DIMENSION

I have been inviting you to look inward. We have peered into our soul, reflected on our life, and dwelled in our mind to deepen our understanding of ourself and our consciousness. Now I want to spend a moment looking *outward,* at the impact you can have on the world around you and what that means for the world-at-large.

You have the ability to help humanity reach its full potential through your actions—to transcend violence, war, trauma, to bring humanity into a greater consciousness. It is essential to engage more frequently in such loving emotions as gratitude, compassion, and ss. Love-based emotions raise your vibrational frequency. Your frequency, whether high or low, affects not only yourself but everyone around you as well. When you are in love-based emotions, you are like a tuning fork, giving those around you a tune-up so they too can live their lives at a higher vibration.

Although you won't see it on the news, there *is* a worldwide shift into higher frequencies taking place. These higher frequencies are attuned with the vibration of love. Higher vibrations raise your consciousness and bring you into an awakened state. It is in this awakened state that our thoughts and actions are driven by love. We not only become more loving, we also develop a deep desire to be in service to others, rather than only being in service to oneself.

Some of those incarnating on the planet right now are born in already awakened states with higher vibrations. There's an excellent reason for that. As Albert Einstein stated, "No problem can be solved from the same level of consciousness that created it." We cannot solve the world's problems and move out of this insanity with the same lower consciousness or mentality. That is why a mass awakening through raised consciousness needs to take place. And it is right now, although you may not feel it because of the ongoing chaos on our planet.

There is tremendous reason for us to have hope for the future. Earth herself is already shifting into a fifth-dimensional existence, a higher vibration. Consequently, all on Gaia are also shifting into these higher frequencies. This is a huge transition, and you want to be a part of it. The assistance from the other side of the veil is unlimited. We have never had this level of angelic assistance. It's now time to break free from the grip of darkness, with its fear and negativity, and become a fifth-dimensional planet of love and compassion.

Our collective consciousness is significantly affected through a unified field, the scientifically proven hundredth-monkey phenomenon. You are part of a movement, a tipping point that is awakening the collective consciousness. Your awakening makes it easier for others to do the same. The angelic realm is working overtime to help you—and everyone else—do just that.

Much is happening beneath the surface to create this worldwide shift into higher consciousness and awakened states. You may have been born a few generations ahead of this shift. If you're already awakened, you may feel that you don't fit in this world. You may also feel you don't fit in with your family. It's not unusual for a more evolved soul to be born into a family of less evolved souls. If this is your reality, it means that you are a path-maker, a pioneer in an evolving "consciousness adjustment."

Ultimately, we are all moving into the love-based fifth dimension of higher vibrations, but some will arrive sooner than others. It's highly likely that you are a forerunner, ahead of the curve. Ask your angels to help you be patient and find peace with others who are in the earlier stages of enlightenment. Use your benevolent guides to help you accept and honor others' choices while they move at their own pace toward higher consciousness.

Continue to allow angels to guide you in *all* areas of your life. Intuitively feel messages from your guardian angels and celestial board of advisors. Follow their suggestions, and your life will be imbued with divine love and power. Closing this book is not the end of something—it is the beginning of a new life. It is the beginning of a new purpose.

☜☞

The Dimensions Explained

*I*t is time for you to go out and begin. But first, let me fully explain what the dimensions are. If you are to get to the fifth dimension—to "vibrate" at this higher level of consciousness—you need to know what's involved and where each new step up this ladder will take you.

What Is a Dimension?

We live in a multidimensional universe. Dimensions are not places or locations; they're levels of consciousness that vibrate at a particular rate. Each dimension, which is a frequency band with a level of reality, vibrates at a higher frequency than the one below. In each higher dimension there exists a clearer, wider perspective of reality, a greater level of knowing. We experience more freedom, greater power, and more opportunity to create our reality. Which level we are a part of and experience depends on our level of spiritual consciousness.

For a higher dimension to be available to us, we need to vibrate in resonance with it. Shifting from one level of consciousness to the next higher one means becoming established on it, so we don't get pulled back.

Those living in third-, fourth-, or fifth-level consciousness are experiencing the same reality on some level, but their way of perceiving it is completely different. Also, it is quite possible to experience multiple dimensions. It is common for some belief systems to still be rooted in third while other aspects are rooted in a higher dimension.

To connect with the angelic realm we need to think outside the 3D box and open our minds to receiving communication from the world higher in vibration to us, the fourth dimension and beyond—the world that surrounds us, where spirits are by our side and yet outside of our world of time and space. Fortunately, we can now get a great deal of help in making the transition to higher vibrations. Benevolent beings from higher dimensional realms are more and more present to assist us. We simply need to ask for their help.

What Is the First Dimension?

The first dimension is an energetic band of vibration that has the lowest frequency. The mineral kingdom resonates at this frequency. The consciousness of this dimension does not possess self-awareness.

What Is the Second Dimension?

The second dimension is an energetic frequency band that vibrates higher than the first dimension. The plants and the lower animal kingdom, such as insects, birds, fish, resonate at this frequency. Consciousness of self-awareness does not exist at this dimension.

What Is the Third Dimension?

The third dimension is the realm of form, the physical reality of conscious beings. The conscious mind of humans and the higher animal kingdom, such as primates, elephants, canines, resonate at this frequency. This dimension is very dense and does not hold as much light as higher dimensions.

In the third dimension the state of consciousness is very restricted. Because we've been living in this third-dimensional reality for so many lifetimes, we tend to assume that this is the only reality available. We think this is simply how reality is, not realizing it's a very narrow experience of reality.

The third dimension runs on rigid beliefs and a fairly inflexible set of rules and limitations. For example, in the third dimension we learn to believe that bodies are solid; they can't merge with one another or walk through walls. Everything is subject to physical rules such as gravity, physical objects cannot disappear, and we cannot read another person's mind. There's a solid belief in duality, and judgment and fear are pervasive.

In the third dimension you see yourself as a separate entity from other people and the universe. You are still rooted in the physical world and feel that it's appropriate to judge people based on the color of their skin, gender, sexual orientation, financial status, etc. Someone considered to be in the third dimension is a person energetically aligned with a frequency with these kinds of third-dimensional perspectives.

What Is the Fourth Dimension?

The fourth dimension is the realm of time. Time is no longer linear in the fourth dimension. There is an ongoing sense of being in present time, with no interest or even awareness of the past and the future. We discover that time is malleable—it can actually stretch and condense.

Manifestation is much faster in the fourth dimension. Something we think about can show up very quickly. In general, when we're experiencing joy, love, and gratitude, we're experiencing fourth-dimensional consciousness.

The fourth dimension is the "bridge" that some of you are in now and will be for a short period of time. In traveling through the fourth dimension, we are preparing ourselves for the fifth dimension.

In fourth-dimensional reality, consciousness begins to awaken. As the light of consciousness begins to awaken within, your belief system concerning third-dimensional reality seems absurd. The attention has shifted from pursuits in the material world to the pursuit of knowledge and understanding. Someone considered to be in the fourth dimension is a person energetically aligned to a frequency with fourth-dimensional perspectives.

Where is this fourth dimension? It's right here, all around us. We do not have to travel to it; it is not separate from the Earth plane by distance or time. It is through a portal or doorway of consciousness that a spirit must pass to enter the fourth dimension. We as humans can step through this doorway by one of two methods. The first is by death of the physical body and the release of the soul. The second is by meditation, astral travel, near-death experiences, or out-of-body experiences. This is when our minds enter an altered state of consciousness and split from our physical bodies.

What Is the Fifth Dimension?

The fifth dimension is the realm of spirit and the unconscious mind. You will encounter what is referred to as "heaven," where souls go when they transition from the third dimension. Souls move out of the dense matter in the third dimension, pierce the veil, and return into higher vibrational energy. In the fifth dimension we will become our higher self, the divine aspect of our self. It is the dimension of love, of living totally from the heart. Someone considered to be in the fifth dimension is a person energetically aligned to the frequency with fifth-dimensional perspectives.

To enter the fifth dimension and stay there, all mental and emotional baggage must be left at the door. No fear, anger, hostility, or guilt exists there; no suffering or sense of separation. As consciousness begins to awaken, the ego drops and judgments begin to fade away.

Mastery over thought is a prerequisite because manifestation in the fifth dimension is instantaneous. When you think about something, it becomes present. People generally communicate through telepathy and have the ability to read one another's thoughts and feelings with ease. The experience of time is radically different: some describe it as everything happening at once. In the fifth dimension there is no distinction between past, present, or future.

Most angels, including archangels and guardian angels, and benevolent spirit guides reside in the fifth dimension. Ascension into even higher dimensions continues after we've reached the fifth.

What Is the Sixth Dimension?

The sixth dimension is a frequency that holds more light. Ascended Masters generally reside in sixth dimension or higher. There are infinite higher dimensions to continue to ascend into vibrationally.

What Is Happening with the Shift in Dimensions?

Earth and all beings living on Earth are in the process of shifting into a whole new level of reality in which the consciousness of love, compassion, peace, and spiritual wisdom prevail. People will be ascending into the fourth and fifth dimensions at their own rate when their frequency is high enough to match the vibration of those higher dimensions.

How Will this Shift Happen?

Thousands of people on the planet are now experiencing an awakening of the heart at an unprecedented rate—and this awakening is speeding up! At some point the collective consciousness will inevitably manifest into a greater consciousness. Those who make the shift with Earth into the fifth dimension will be going through some intense changes, as their bodies and minds make the transformations needed to shift into the higher consciousness required for moving into the fifth dimension.

Glossary

angels: Conscious celestial beings who exist in a higher-vibrational dimension, usually the fifth dimension; they often act as messengers for Divine Source

archangel: An angel who is a leader in the celestial planes

Ascended Master: An enlightened being who has attained spiritual transformation, generally resides in the sixth dimension or higher frequencies; they have previously lived as a human

celestial being: An entity from the ethers, heavens, or higher-vibrational dimension, usually referring to an angel

divine: Of, from, or like God/Goddess

divine nature: The characteristics and traits of Divine Source, God/Goddess; our true, authentic essence

Divine Source: God/Goddess, the origin and essence of all life

fifth dimension: An energetic frequency band that vibrates higher than the fourth dimension; this dimension of love has a level of consciousness of living totally from the heart (see appendix, The Dimensions Explained)

fourth dimension: An energetic frequency band that vibrates higher than the third dimension; the fourth dimension has a level of consciousness of spiritual awakening and heart-opening experiences (see appendix, The Dimensions Explained)

God/Goddess: A deity, the source and essence of all life

guardian angel: A benevolent spiritual being who watches over and protects someone

higher consciousness: A state of elevated awareness where a person has a deeper understanding of the true nature of reality, which enables fuller self-realization and enlightenment

higher self: The real you that is unlimited, eternal, conscious, and your highest aspect (same as *oversoul*)

higher-vibrational dimension: A plane of existence with increased energy frequency (see appendix, The Dimensions Explained)

meditation: Quieting your mind's thoughts and turning your focus inward, becoming more present and mindful

medium: A person who communicates directly with spirits

Mother Mary: The mother of Jesus and an Ascended Master

oversoul: Same as the higher self

reincarnation: The soul's rebirth in a new body

soul: Eternal essence and animating principle that inhabits the body and acts through it

spirit guides: The disincarnated spirit of a soul in a higher-vibrational dimension, usually the fifth dimension, who guides and assists an incarnated soul having a human experience

third dimension: An energetic frequency band that vibrates at a certain rate, lower than the fourth or fifth dimensions; the third dimension has a level of consciousness that is very limited and restricted (see appendix, The Dimensions Explained)

veil: An invisible division between our world on Earth and other dimensions; when we incarnate in a human body, we pass through the veil, which greatly limits our consciousness and awareness

Index

ABOUT THE AUTHORS

ROBBIE HOLZ

Robbie's life was drastically altered in 1985 when, after a difficult thirty-six-hour delivery while giving birth to her only child, she was given a blood transfusion to "perk her up faster." Unfortunately, the transfusion was tainted with hepatitis C. Since Western medicine was no longer able to help her, Robbie set out to find alternative ways to survive and recover. She ultimately healed herself of hepatitis C, fibromyalgia, chronic fatigue syndrome, and treatment-induced temporary brain damage, described in her award-winning memoir, *Aboriginal Secrets of Awakening*.

While on her quest for wellness, Robbie met Dr. Gary Holz, an award-winning physicist, psychoneuroimmunologist, and alternative healer. The two eventually married. Gary taught her the native healing techniques he learned from his encounter with remote aboriginal tribespeople in the Australian Outback, chronicled in his best-selling memoir, *Secrets of Aboriginal Healing*.

Like her husband, Robbie has had firsthand experiences with aboriginal tribespeople in the Australian Outback. She joined Gary in teaching the over 60,000-year-old aboriginal healing system, revealed to the world at the tribe's request. Starting in 1997, their healing practice centered on aboriginal healing principles, quantum physics, and psychoneuroimmunology—using the mind to heal the body.

Robbie is an award-winning author, internationally respected healer and speaker, and remains dedicated to helping people worldwide. She has also worked widely as a medium, helping countless people connect to the other side. She hopes this book, *Angels in Waiting*, will awaken more of us to develop a connection with our angels and spirit guides and to use their tremendous help.

Today Robbie lives in the Pacific Northwest. She is currently writing a companion workbook to *Angels in Waiting*. Her website is **www.holzwellness.com**.

JUDY KATZ

Judy Katz has ghostwritten, edited, published, and publicized forty-four books and counting. Among her many successful endeavors, Judy's greatest passion in life is helping people tell their inspiring stories, assisting aspiring authors to become successful, sought-after authors and speakers.

Judy graduated from the University of California, Berkeley, where she had her own column, "Meaning's Edge," in the *Daily Californian* for four years. She wrote for a medical advertising agency and two McGraw Hill magazines before consecutively becoming public relations director of Madison Square Garden, the New York March of Dimes, and the National Multiple Sclerosis Society.

A true entrepreneur, Judy then established and managed her own public relations firm, Katz Creative, Inc. In 2002, she founded the ghostwriting division of Katz Creative, Inc.

Judy has a publishing arm, New Voices Press, and along with offering self-publishing services she helps promote her authors' books to serve them as "the ultimate marketing and reputation-building tool."

For her, *Angels in Waiting* was more than just another writing or editing project. In the course of working with Robbie Holz, she notes, "I connected with my guardian angel and my celestial board of advisors. When I asked for their help, in the ways in which Robbie instructs us to ask, my life took an extraordinary turn that came from outside what we know of as reality, but what I discovered is only the tip of the iceberg."

Judy is a proud member of the Authors Guild, PEN America, and many other prestigious professional and networking organizations. Her website is **www.katzcreativebooksandmedia.com**. She can also be found on LinkedIn and Facebook. Judy can be reached at (212) 580-8833 or **jkatzcreative@gmail.com**.